Nature Kindergartens and Forest Schools

An exploration of naturalistic learning within Nature Kindergartens and Forest Schools

Claire Warden

Many thanks to all the children and adults who have made this book possible.
Special thanks to Mum, Ivy Campion, who channelled the wildness in me.

Design and layout by Niki Buchan
Photography by Niki Buchan, Claire Warden and the Kindergarten teams
All photographs © Mindstretchers Ltd

ISBN 978-1-906116-09-5

If you would like training materials or in-service on this book
please contact Mindstretchers Ltd
www.claire-warden.com

Mindstretchers Ltd
Glenruthven Mill
Abbey Road
Auchterarder
Perthshire
PH3 1DP
Scotland
United Kingdom
Tel: +44(0)1764 664409
Fax: +44(0)1764 660728
Email: enquiries@mindstretchers.co.uk
www.mindstretchers.co.uk

Foreword

'One does not set out in search of new lands without being willing to be alone on an empty sea'.

André Gide

Every now and then a little treasure comes along that celebrates the child and childhood. This book is just that little bit of gold dust. It is warm, passionate, yet strong and brave and will support you on your ongoing journey wherever it may lead. Be prepared to be awakened.

Claire begins by sharing her vision of the Nature Kindergartens. Here, she presents her view of the child as a capable, competent and trustworthy individual. This ontological view is threaded throughout the book, emerging in waves from other discussions, seamlessly and intrinsically. There is a sense of a drive to achieve a transformation of education in Scotland by providing a more coherent, flexible and enriched natural curriculum, advocating children not as sole leaders of their learning, but within an equilibrium where children and adults together negotiate, where children are listened to and encouraged to apply their own logic to any given situation, rather than trying to impress on them our adult intellect. The word 'respect' surfaces often as does 'consultation', respect for the child as a natural, active learner who should be consulted throughout the ongoing process of learning.

A sense of community among the child, their family, staff members and the wider social world is a key aspect of the life of the kindergartens. The focus of working together is embedded in everyday practice; the sharing of bread baked by members of the community, for example, brings everyone together. Resourcing indoors reflects the outdoors, with simple, unrefined resources, natural materials from the floor of the forest, or wooden blocks for construction. These simple resources support open-ended play opportunities, both indoors and outdoors. (Importantly Claire reminds us that open ended materials do not 'need' to be natural, but she does place high importance on the ethical and sustainable use of resources, and the visual harmony needed). This connection with spaces is essential, as Claire suggests because we separate children's worlds when we take them to outdoor spaces, rather than connect the two places. 'When allowed to 'be' in natural spaces, she explains, 'children will invariably astound us with the ideas and situations they create, humbling us into remembering the pure joy of childhood when you could be and do anything you wanted'.

She argues that children are naturally connected to nature, they see the detail in it, they listen to it, they move with it. Claire places great importance on adults' attitudes and understanding, because she believes with these, skills and knowledge can be taught. Traditionally-trained adults are often keen to 'fill in the oracy gaps,' but there are times when learning continues without words.

This book encourages us to look at the beautiful natural landscapes around us, truly listen to the child, with all our senses, and have no expectations of what will be. The child within nature will be the guide of what will, or can happen and that whatever happens is the way it should be. And we should trust that.

We are reminded that legacies of the past have much to teach us. It is true to say that the main principles of Froebel, Montessori and Steiner have not lost their validity, in fact they are in advance of a great deal of current practice, as Claire informs the reader of the connections to current early years environments. There are many signposts throughout; research from both historical and current perspectives and from many local and global contexts 'informs' this book. It may be that the reader wishes to pursue these in more detail; again Claire plants the seed, not leading you, not directing you, but encouraging you on your journey.

As I read this book I found myself reflecting on my own childhood, the frisson of swinging on a rope across a stream, that wonderful feeling that has never left me, reflecting on my time with my own children, when they were young, as Mischa, my daughter, brought me a beetle (a very ugly beetle) she found 'lost' in the garden, encouraging us to look for the rest of its family, and reflecting on my practice today, when children celebrate the natural world with a look on their face of awe and wonder as a robin pops down to say hello. I am putting this book down now; no doubt I will return to it many times. I am left with 'magical thoughts' of my own. Hopefully it will open up your thinking and encourage you to take a leap of faith, follow your dream and believe in what is true.

Lynn McNair O.B.E
Cowgate under 5's Centre
Edinburgh
Scotland
United Kingdom

Contents

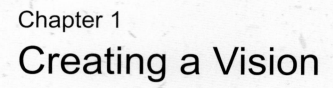

Chapter 1
Creating a Vision

'Tell me...What is it you plan to do with your one wild and precious life?'

Mary Oliver

The journey started several years ago when I received a phone call from a lovely person called Sarah. As a mother, she was looking for someone to support a local nursery to prevent its closure. My great 'Life Plan' had not included the development and implementation of a methodology. Sometimes life has a way of unfolding, and for me these forays have afforded a wealth of wonderful experiences across the globe. So, after a meeting with a group of parents we decided to develop the centre as our definition of a Nature Kindergarten linked to models seen in parts of Scandinavia and Europe.

The term Nature Kindergarten has come to stand for our definition and approach of naturalistic, wild spaces that provide children with a landscape in which to play for very long blocks of time. The approach or methodology about how you work with them in that space is as important and has key aspects that we consider to be effective and essential to our definition. A summary of the key aspects of Nature Kindergarten are defined in each chapter of this book. The Nature Kindergarten journey and this book that stems from it, are personal to me. I would like the concept to be personal for you too and to this end, each chapter has some key points to think about or for you to follow on your journey.

Our decision to create a centre was an absolute conviction that 'natural' spaces both in terms of resources, environments and the mentoring skills of the staff are the most effective and appropriate for children. The more I see, the more it makes you reflect on what is defined as high quality childcare. As I travel the world listening to practitioners who work in a variety of spaces, with a variety of children and their families, I developed an opinion that some of the western traditions developing in childcare and education are not always the best for the inner child.

These are the values I use to underpin the approach we have:

• Small numbers of children in home styled spaces
The rise of large centres with hundreds of children on roll concerns me for both the emotional aspects of the children but also how the relationship develops with the families they come from, so we decided to create centres akin to children's houses, small units of no more than twenty children in local spaces, so that the link within the local community is supported and in some cases developed. The houses are set up to be just that, small units with cosy spaces, often with log stoves for heat, blankets and slippers make the lodges homely places with direct year round access to wild spaces, everyday.

• Mixed age group sessions
The children work in family groups with 2-5 years old in the same group, this creates what I feel is a more 'normal' way to learn. Family units have the natural age range and give the children a buffer zone where they can be 'emotionally polished' to smooth off some of the aspects and behaviours that do not suit a community based space. The apprenticeship approach to learning has been used for a long time in education and is very effective as long as all children within it experience challenge in their thinking.

• Community hub
In some instances when families do not have extended family around them, urban lifestyles can actually lead to some isolation if there is no common meeting place. Day care of children whether playgroup, family centres, toddler groups or nurseries offers this forum for parents and carers to network and become involved in the community of the centre - a 'fellowship' as Froebel would have said. We decided to offer social experiences such as felt making classes, jewellery making, construction days, eco-days or family sessions for adults to create connections, both within nursery but also at weekends, holidays and evenings.

• Open ended resources in visually simple spaces

The rise of overdesigned resources with too small a role for creativity can lead to children who are too prescribed in their thinking. The ability to vocalise and reflect, to inspire, to problem solve are attributes that have come from a place where children have been given some autonomy and the space 'to think outside the box', both in terms of curriculum and the spaces they are in. The resources we put into the centres are flexible and open ended that ensures they have multiple uses across the curriculum, the spaces are defined after watching children and their play behaviours so that the organisation of the space makes sense to the children using it. For example the play dough or clay goes into a role play area or as a medium for connecting blocks or modelling characters to use in small worlds both inside and out.

• Risk full learning

The most complex hazards are removed in the nature kindergartens, but the risk remains. The development of a risk adverse society is creating what Tim Gill calls the 'shrinking horizons of childhood' where the independence and freedom of childhood has been curtailed. If we listen to experts from other parts of the world such as America, we find Richard Louv talking of the 'criminalisation of natural play' through public response to children playing in a stream. On the other side of the world we find Sue Elliot who is supporting the development of naturalistic spaces in Australia. The global aspect of the work I now do provides me with the wonderful opportunity to meet the children and these people across the globe. There is a global trend towards risk aversion, but alongside it is a tenacious group of people fighting for a child's right to feel 'the knot in the stomach', the adrenalin, when you start to move out of the comfort zone. The naturalistic spaces are first and foremost for the children, their experiences outside have inspired many people to reflect on their own provision no matter how small or urbanised.

• Eco friendly and sustainable living

The rise of plastic and especially unrecyclable plastic materials has been a concern for the company for some time. The increase in Local Authority funding lead to a rapid advance in the amount of plastic equipment in centres that in the cause of technology are designed to ping and 'whirr'. There are two aspects of this that concern me. Firstly, is the environmental impact where the amount of plastic going into landfill sites is truly staggering. Given that the children using the resources are going to be the ones facing the waste minimisation and handling it is only right that we start to ask questions on their behalf so that the earth is still beautiful in sixty years time. Where do broken resources from educational spaces go? Do people ask about the disposal options when they buy a resource? Our approach has risen out of an ecological awareness. It almost passes as a given that all the Nature Kindergartens hold a green eco school status. For international readers this is a quality indicator in Scottish education that ensures that centres work in environmentally aware communities, encouraging children to reduce waste, power use, litter, water use and promote sustainability, healthy eating, biodiversity and the use of school grounds.

Secondly, the closed resources often have very limited play affordance and therefore flexibility to the learner. If too much emphasis is placed on the artificiality of materials, trying to replicate reality, I would question why not just use real materials. In most cases they are far more sustainable, especially if they have had a natural evolution, for instance wooden wheels.

• Fair Trade

If one looks at education on a global basis then it is only right that young children in one part of the world are not making the toys for children in another. All the resources within the Nature Kindergartens are not only recyclable but also fair trade and ethically sourced. Through this work the children link to the person behind the product, not simply the brash commercialism so often seen in children's lives.

• Physicality

Children need to be more active. I was recently at a talk by leading specialists at Yorkhill Children's Hospital in Glasgow. Their research was conducted by gathering data from pedometers to see how active children are. The results stated that children do not move enough. It went on to state that 1 in 10 children are clinically obese. The type of food they are eating has far too many hidden sugars, and although the calorific content has dropped over the last 20 years, the sedentary lifestyle has lead to an increase in stored fat. Even without this research to back up the approach, informed adults know how important movement is to a child. The feeling of being exhausted, is not something to avoid, but rather something to be experienced as the result of an active, often risk filled play session. In order to be active, the Nature Kindergarten indoor areas have few sedentary spaces, and those that are present are able to be put down/up or used in various ways as required. The children can be outside for the whole session or for a minimum of 6 hours (daily total) in all weathers, all year round. The physical aspects of their development are promoted through running, climbing trees, and physically being in wide open spaces with a canopy of trees for a roof.

• Consideration of inner and outer health

The food we eat at Nature Kindergarten is wholesome. Children are encouraged to cook and explore new foods. Current research suggests that children may need 10 to 15 attempts to taste a food to develop a preference. There is a strong link between cooking and the produce that is grown in the garden area. Organic vegetable and fruit boxes are used to supplement the diet in the leaner months. The presence of a Kinder Kitchen on one of the sites enables children to make their own food such as bread, everyday. The food tunnel on an adjacent site enables children to harvest fruit, berries and vegetables in the season that nature intended. The wild food that we gather is identified by informed adults so that children see that some food is for the wildlife and some for humans.

The emphasis placed on physical health is often higher than mental health, our inner health. In times of emotional turbulence we are so influenced by our inner feelings that it can become a physical pain. The Nature Kindergartens look at the whole child, often building high emotional resilience that children can use through life. Self image increases when we let nature in because it offers emotional harmony and visual calmness, its open ended experiences are affirming and with that framework, all other aspects of development may move forward more easily.

• Children as motivated thinkers

The approach I have adhered to for the whole of my teaching career, despite changes in curriculum documents and policy, has been the fact that children need a connection to the learning and should be inspired and motivated by the process. My book entitled Talking and Thinking Floorbooks has been wonderfully popular in changing people's attitudes and

upgrading interaction skills so that discussions and reflections, not just question and answer sessions, are at the root of learning connections. To feel valued as a human being we need to feel listened to. Children should be consulted so that they are part of the learning process, after all, it is their life. The Nature Kindergartens use this Floorbook planning and many examples of a group's learning journeys are held within this book. Indeed, I feel that the skill of working outside for long blocks of time is linked to the ability to respond to children. The second aspect of planning is that the contexts should be purposeful to young children. Children have a fascination with the world around them and this can supply the adults with so many possible lines of enquiry that nature offers the framework of learning. Children can spend weeks exploring the idea of a fire and what it needs to 'breathe', or we can work through repeated visits to the Floorbooks over a year to record ideas about the growth of a particular plant.

• Children as capable and competent

Assessment is an integral part of teaching and learning and should therefore 'be integrated'. There are a number of programmes for the assessment of children that separate learning from experience. I truly believe that children need to be heard within a space where they are comfortable, in order to really reflect their capacity and level of thinking. The guide through a child's learning journey should be themselves with an adult there as support, in order to learn we need to revisit that learning in a process called meta cognition so that our brains can understand what it is we didn't know. The children at the Nature Kindergartens have time to show us what they know. Recording systems are child friendly so that assessment is formative and they are an integral part of the summative process. Observations take place outside as well as some group experiences such as 3D mind mapping, which involves the use of objects taken from a 'talking tub' and used to provocate thinking. The processes allow children time to make connections and consider the knowledge and awareness they already hold and are on the pathway to develop further.

• Trust in their self preservation

Children are capable in many ways. If we trust children to be empowered so that they can choose to use real materials then it is important that we do actually trust them and not stand hovering waiting for the accident. I do not believe that children would want to drown in a puddle or use a rope around their neck, because I trust my judgement and that of the child. There will always be a few children that you know need more support and care, but not all children should have their lives restricted by the specialist care for one.

• Respect for children – their views, differences and levels of ability

Adults need to truly listen and respond to children. Adults need to be fully present and mindful of people in the time and space they are in. It is really interesting to explore cultures around the world to sense how they treat the youngest and oldest members, since these groups can become marginalised and devalued as citizens. Children have opinions from an early age and we as adults should pay credence to them, since they enable us to create a close match in provision.

Chapter 2
Why a Nature Kindergarten?

'Together we have enough resources and tools to provide children with a space to dream'.

Christina Noble

The time is right to start to talk about naturalised outdoor learning but with that increased interest comes the huge increase in terminology and variances in approach. As a Nature Kindergarten founder, a Forest School Leader, a consultant and as a parent, I am hugely committed to taking children to nature outside – in whatever guise that may be, but also bringing nature to them, both in school grounds and inside their space. Children have always been connected to nature. It is so often the adults around them who have lost the link.

There are existing educational models that have common threads running through them, some examples would be 'Ich ur o skur', translated to Rain or Shine Nurseries, Sweden, 'Skogsmulle' are run across Scandinavia, similar to our Forest School but can also be delivered by scout groups, 'Metsämörri', are Finland's own version of 'Skogsmulle', 'Udeskole', are Denmark's version of Forest Schools for 7-16 years olds. Each variation has differences in terms of time spent outside, the structure afforded to the session and the age focus. All these models have to be set within the cultural framework from which it has formed. The Scandinavian approach to the outdoors, referred to as 'friluftsliv', encompasses a cultural way of life and would warrant further reading to fully understand it. It is certainly seen as deep rooted and connected to a cultural norm.

Our decision was linked to the vision of a 'natural children's garden' with all the aspects that it encompasses from the landscape, to the food, the materials and resources used and the sense of community within it, but also the natural desire to have ones voice heard and valued from a very early stage.

So why nature? Well, the research is wide ranging and from all parts of the globe, to support its use on multiple levels. Here is a summary of some of the research and their findings that have affirmed our values.

• Children who play regularly in natural environments show more advanced motor fitness, including coordination, balance and agility, and they are sick less often (Grahn, et al. 1997, Fjortoft & Sageie 2001).

• When children play in natural environments, their play is more diverse with imaginative and creative play that fosters language and collaborative skills (Moore & Wong 1997, Taylor, et al. 1998, Fjortoft 2000).

• Exposure to natural environments improves children's cognitive development by improving their awareness, reasoning and observational skills (Pyle 2002).

• Spending time in nature has been shown to reduce stress and benefit treatment of numerous health conditions (Kahn 1999).

• Nature buffers the impact of life's stresses on children and helps them deal with adversity. The greater the amount of nature exposure, the greater the benefits (Wells & Evans 2003).

• Children with Attention Deficit Disorder are positively affected by the calmness of natural playscapes (Taylor et al 2001).

• An affinity to and love of nature, along with a positive environmental ethic, grow out of regular contact with and play in the natural world during early childhood. (Chawla 1998; Sobel 1996,2002, 2004; Wilson 1997; Moore and Cosco, 2000; Kals et al 1999, 2003).

- Early experiences with the natural world have been positively linked with the development of imagination and the sense of wonder (Cobb 1977, Louv 1991).

- Wonder is an important motivator for life long learning (Wilson 1997).

- Children who play in nature have more positive feelings about each other (Moore 1986).

- Natural environments stimulate social interaction between children (Moore 1986, Bixler et al. 2002).

It is very apparent from all the research that young children have a natural connection to nature and will seek and find nature in even the most unlikely places. A little girl of two was playing in a parking area and her attention was held by something along the wall. The adult approached and she turned round and silently pointed at something in the hole she had been creating amongst the bricks and rubble. A woodlouse.

With two fingers she gently lifted it out and placed it on the driveway where she prodded it and silently watched it walk away. During this encounter she was fully engaged in the activity and the movements from the bit of nature she found in a concrete gap.

So, given that we know through research that children need nature, do they need it all the time, for an hour or two, or for 15 minutes, and in what guise should 'nature' be offered? The minimum should be daily and then for a long block so that they relax and settle into the space. The rise of Forest School has been exciting, my first contact with Gordon Woodall from Bridgewater College and Sally York from the Forestry Commission in Scotland, was over 10 years ago to discuss the possibilities of the use of local woodlands through 'Forest Schools'. At that point the journey had hardly begun, although rangers have been working in woodlands with children it did not have the widespread, integrated approach currently being attempted. The balance of knowledge in nature based programmes interests me. The position of that 'knowledge' defines how the programmes work. If the ranger holds it, it seems to affect the way the educator interacts with the children on the site, if the educator is skilled and knowledgeable about the natural space and how to be in it, then their interaction and transfer of experience to the centre is far more embedded in what they do. In the United Kingdom teachers and practitioners have found 'ring fenced' time for a half day session, once a week, for a number of weeks for children to travel to a woodland site to attend Forest School. Although not required, many Forest School Leaders have taken additional qualifications to develop outdoor skills, and rangers are raising their knowledge of educational models. There is still a difference between this methodology and Nature Kindergartens, as we define them, since the daily connection to a wild space ensures a real sharing of knowledge between the adult and child without the third relationship of the other adult.

In some cases, unfortunately, the agenda for Forest School type sessions are often set by the adult so that a programme is drawn up to develop skills, or knowledge that can then be applied to a project such as a shelter, fire and so forth. There can be a flexibility between weeks, although most schools adhere to a programme once it is set.

It is at this point that I see the early years as having a different model. It is here that we have defined our style of Nature Kindergarten, to meet the need of the children, families and overarching education system in the UK. The younger the child the more responsive and fluid I think we need to be, so that they can develop skills within a purposeful context over several consecutive days. For a two year old, the space of a week is actually a long time to carry forward shared thinking. The Nature Kindergartens spend from 70 to 100 per cent of their time outside, flowing from day to day exploring subtle changes in nature as a small family group.

Early years centres in Scotland will no longer be commissioned if they do not have access to an outside space, which is wonderful news. However, the variety of styles and designs of outdoor access in terms of quality is huge. All have the potential for a naturalised space even if very small. The landscape is only half of the story, it is our methodology of creating a nature kindergarten that must have a higher level of child consultation, shared thinking and integration and access to wild, natural spaces inside and out, for all children. The integration of all the elements brings a synergy to the style of care that would be lost if only small aspects were taken on board.

Trees do give a real sense of place, being surrounded by objects that are older than you, that will be here long after you have gone actually provides an amazing grounding for all human beings. Given that many parts of Scotland do not have a woodland space, but do have stunning shores and mountains, it seemed exclusive rather than inclusive to use the term Forest Kindergartens. I am delighted to see the rise in any approach to taking children outside. However, unless they support a change of methodology they

may also simply become a forest school, but with younger children who have a weekly activity session in the forest, this is not the same as a Nature Kindergarten.

The methodology of our Nature Kindergartens is that nature creates the context and the curriculum comes from it in a more natural way than over planned activity driven days. It can be achieved in any space, a meadow, seashore, stream, hill, desert, frozen waste, it doesn't need to be a forest, although trees are wonderful for shelter there are other ways. What lies at our root are all the aspects listed in Chapter 1, they come together to create a naturalistic space with a way of working with children that is consultative, where risk taking is encouraged and there is a consistency of access that creates a real link for children. Many children are not 'allowed' the freedom to explore, test themselves in play and to feel in control of being 'out of control'. When play behaviours are restricted the drive from the human is to find another way to achieve play goals. In the nature kindergartens we have slopes, some of them steep, it is important that children feel the sensation of being in control of being out of control as they run down them. To put too many restrictions on this actually takes away the learning moment for the emotional intelligence of the child.

The following chapters will take the reader through some of the subtle aspects of developing one of our nature kindergartens. The content is designed to be thought provoking and yet affirming since children have shown us over the years, that it is the root things in life that really matter.

Key Points:

Nature Kindergartens have a different framework and methodology in our work to other approaches to nature based learning across the world.

Nature Kindergartens as we have defined them are linked to a way of 'being' with children and creating care and education for them.

Nature based learning both inside and out works in a more harmonious way with young children on all aspects of their development.

Chapter 3
A place where children are capable, competent learners

'Children know what is interesting when they see it'.

Robert Pyle

How do you see learning? Should we define it as a life long journey that never stops until the day you depart? Is it a feast of excitement full of passion and rigour? A process rather than a product related activity? Or, is it a confusing and slightly uncomfortable experience as you move out of your comfort zone? The lists and adjectives at our fingertips to define perceptions of learners and their learning are truly staggering. And yet there are people who, although able to verbalise, still hold a traditional view of the child as a blank canvas. In order to further dismiss that notion, we have come to this point in the book where we are going to reassert the many movements in education that hold the view that children are competent, capable learners. The development of people's perceptions of the learning process within themselves, and the children that they teach, have evolved over time. Adults are influenced in their thinking by their experience, but also by people around them who have come to define their ideas and values like Froebel, Pestalozzi, Montessori, Steiner and a small group of pedagogista in the region of Reggio Emelia.

Froebel (1782-1852), came from a background of forestry and as such the connection of child led, nature based experiences were at the core of his work. The views he held on the role of play in learning endures all this time later. Froebel initiated the use of the word Kindergarten to emphasise the 'children's garden' and how vital it was in those early stages of being. Froebel looked to nature to provide resources and objects for learning both inside and out, abstract blocks, hollowed bowls, stone counters were all considered as 'gifts'. Through his work with Pestalozzi (1746-1827), the movement of Steiner education started to evolve in Germany in the early Twentieth Century.

Steiner education brought together values to honour and protect 'the wonder' of childhood. The adult is a guide rather than a director creating environments that support exploration and investigation such as those clearly found in natural Kindergartens. Steiner supported the development of risk taking so that children were encouraged to push themselves in their play, which he felt was a natural phenomenon, curbed only by adults. The children who enter the nature kindergartens have the benefit of 'slow' pacing within a daily visited space, small boundaries of extension that enable them to move outward from their comfort zone. Forest School programmes that work on weekly cycles would find it hard to achieve this since they move between two worlds of more formal education and the wild spaces of nature. In the northern European communities, the place of Steiner can be seen through the Waldkindergarten or 'forest children's garden'. In Scandinavian countries, for example Norway, we see 'friluftsliv', or 'outdoor/fresh air life' embedded in wider cultural constructs of family and society. Attitudes to the learning process and the place of risk within it vary between nations, yet all are influential in our practice. I will return to these thoughts in Chapter 5.

The emphasis in the work of Steiner schools is also that of spirituality. There are moments were many adults have spoken of some form of spirituality when in a wilder space. The sense of who you are in a larger frame is certainly never clearer than when in a space where you feel like a speck, gazing into stars or being buffeted by strong winds, does create a sense of the size of the natural space and how irrelevant humans actually are within it.

Creativity and make-believe was central to the work of Steiner and the emphasis on the sensorial engagement fits closely to the work taking place in natural spaces across the globe. As a heightened awareness of nature based education builds, it is wonderful to see countries such as Nepal as the richer counterparts to urbanised American in areas such as down town New York. The work through action research sites such as the World Forum for Education, has enabled practitioners to create networks and cross borders more effectively than any national strategy to see lands as nature rich.

The first Nature Kindergarten we developed had been based on Maria Montessori's philosophies. The place of nature in Montessori's work was connected to the origins in the slums of Rome, where the availability of nature was the saving element in terms of both economics and the application of her ideas across all countries in the world. Montessori used repetition for consolidation, which has been carried forward into our work. There is however no defined 'work time' since the children are constantly working on ideas and theories to make sense of the world around them. They do naturally seek out repetition of climbing a certain log, or lining up the fir cones on a set stone in the forest. The place of the individual is also of note. The presentation of the abstract has some order inside the centres; sensorial mathematical materials in our work are presented on wooden trays that are used indoors and outdoors. The presentation of the natural materials is important for us both inside and outside in the garden area, nature creates its own presentation style in the wild space. The organisational elements that Montessori developed through practical life skills have evolved. How to put on a pair of waterproof trousers; sequencing a cooking activity to make bread; tending and caring for plants; polishing muddy shoes and taking care of the centre both inside and in the garden are all positive elements of our work.

On a recent study trip to Reggio, it was significant to see the effect of Montessori on the development of a style of educational movement that undoubtedly affected Loris Malaguzzi. The community he worked within was made up of strong women who wished to go to work, the funding and support from the municipality of Reggio Emilia and pedagogues who had views of the child led to a shifting pattern of educational values that is now shared across the world. The pedagogues belief in the child as competent, the environment as the third teacher and the place of creativity in learning to enable the multiple possibilities of interpretation are all closely connected to the outdoor space - nature. In reality the journey for the centres to be outside for long blocks of time is affected by a strong cultural view in Italy that the weather can affect your health. Nature is used as provocation, but in most centres visited, it comes from adults presenting it to children inside the outdoor rooms that are enclosed for most of the year by folding glass doors. In the centres visited, journeys outside this are made for short blocks of time and for physical experiences on climbing frames. The pedagogista who link the centres, felt that it was part of their ongoing journey, to support the centres to be outside for greater parts of the year.

In Lombardy in northern Italy, we found an approach where the director of education is supporting the state schools to play outside. In these centres, there was evidence that children play outside in their garden areas on a frequent basis. They work closely with the local farm schools to extend the experience for children over a number of visits over a number of weeks. The agricultural area has a network of farmers who have created areas on the farm for children to come to and work with nature. The farmers' feedback to us was that the children need time to get into the rhythm to really link to the natural space they are in, otherwise it is just an 'activity'. The experiences are targeted so each farm has a specialism such as sweet corn, arable (bread), bees, fruit or olives. On our journey we found a farm to harvest honey, to use it in baking and to stimulate stories about positive ways to sweeten food and then to use the bees wax to sculpt and make candles. The experience certainly widens children's awareness of their place within the community and culture of the region. It does give a real sense of where the food they eat comes from, but it does not hold the educational aspects of play based learning.

Throughout all of these approaches, in some cases idealist concepts about the child and their 'innate' learning drive, there are consistent threads of key moments or a trigger - Joseph Clinton Pearce (1977), talks of magical moments. The Reggio group (2009), refers to nodes of learning whilst Chawla (1990), refers to 'radioactive jewels'. Wordsworth (quoted in Chawla 2002), talks of the experience of 'spots of time'. What links them all together is an emotional shift, which in turn may have a new learning direction. The direction may be a deepening, an altered course to an associated concept, or perhaps an affirmation of group cohesiveness. Direction of learning is multi-faceted and multi-directional, it is this aspect that educators need to hold onto in their work within the bigger frame of the educational culture of their country. Where forest programmes, visits to parks or nature education programmes become part of a schedule, a list of activities or events may appear that does not give the space for magical moments to emerge to become threads of enquiry. It is almost as if there is a mistrust of nature that can make us feel the need to guarantee an experience. The discoveries that will occur and the way they are documented must take into account the flexibility of the learning process.

The cultural and climatic effects on the approaches above are also worthy of note. The emphasis for the Norwegian culture is to be outside, the other approaches went outside. There is a subtle difference in that to 'be' somewhere is to work on another plane. It takes time to be mindful and present when you are in the space. To go outside can be at a more transient nature, to use it, play there and then go back inside.

The context of the learning environment over the whole year is outdoors for Pearce, indoors on the whole in Reggio Emelia, and so when we look in depth, the largest amount of time traditionally spent outside is in the outdoor nurseries, or nature schools set up all over Europe in the 18th Century.

The effect on learning of these moments cannot be measured over a day or a year but over a life time. Wordsworth spoke of the spots of time coming together to create unforgettable experiences where children "do not yet differentiate themselves from their surroundings". Adults often recall, and draw inspiration from, such magical experiences in natural settings as the strongest, most powerful memories of childhood. Some of our greatest inventors spent long blocks of time exploring nature, albeit trying to harness it in terms of Edison, or overtaking its geographical spread for Alexander Graham Bell. Artists have been inspired by it, Renoir, Constable, Monet all comment on 'natures light' in their work.

Some of the research linked to human connections to nature seems to be coming from people in outdoor education and environmental education who have themselves gone through hazardous, risk-full experiences. There is a movement of educators that are connecting to the essence of the experience and trying to find ways to change the perhaps more traditional, outdoor adventurer genre of 'I will conquer nature', into a more connected way so that the journey starts on the walk to the river, not just the adrenaline pumping rapids to canoe. Colin Mortlock (2000), describes his feelings of connectedness rather than his mastery of the space. It was 'as if I were part of the ocean environment...accepting fully that everything around me was somehow related to, and part of me. It was the deepest feeling of peace and harmony'.

Co-operative learning or collaborative learning is a process and teaching strategy whereby small teams, each with children of different levels of ability or age, use a variety of learning activities to improve their understanding of a subject. Key aspects include positive interdependence, face to face interactions, individual and group accountability, interpersonal and small group skills and group processing. All of the aspects detailed should be present in the nature kindergarten. Woven into the experience has to lie independence to choose where to go, whether to climb or not. Children are encouraged from an early stage to have conversations with each other and with staff so that oracy is given a high status as a learning method. Meetings are called to explore group accountability to discuss why all the paintbrushes are all out of shape. Children are held accountable through the allocation of roles, feeding back their actions, creating something or teaching others what they have learned. Settled times explore the interpersonal skills that are so vital for a learning community. The Talking and Thinking Floorbooks™, we use in our work bring together both individual and group processing to allow children to learn but also to revisit and consolidate.

The key to the work in kindergartens is that the children create 'community' without an over directive adult. The social interaction skills develop in a natural way, since the outdoor space does not contain levels of expectation or set ways of working that may well get in the way of group dynamics. The centres are set up to celebrate 'family' in all its forms. Younger children are supported by older children or indeed children who are more skilled than they, or perhaps more knowledgeable so the dynamics of support vary from context to context, day to day.

When visiting the Waldkindergarten in Germany, we recognised how we, so often in our practice, "gather" children. The schedule for these children involved being dropped off at one of the shelter points in a public wood. There was shelter and seating that children came to and then left again over the space of the day or session. The space that pulled them in was a dip about a metre deep at its deepest point, approximately 3 metres across.

The photograph shown here gives a wonderful indication of the diverse experiences taking place, physically located together with very clear 'individual pathways' coming through.

These children engaged in sky watching, whittling, singing, bouncing on a green sapling, leaning on a tree to chat and deep level conversations about their piece of wood being used as a laser gun. The adult was away from the group, but

very aware of their presence and whether the conversation was 'healthy', not calm and unchallenging but not too biased to one child or another. There was an acceptance of disagreement.

Many years ago, I was a trustee of a charity called 'The Speygrian', it was set up by Joyce Gilbert in Scotland, after the concept of a journey experienced in Canada. The approach was designed to bring together groups of people including artists, musicians, poets, educators from all over the country to share a journey. On my first trip as a participant we went together on fully rigged sailing ship around Mull, an island off the west coast of Scotland, as part of a training week. The experience of learning together to be in more remote spaces was a bonding experience. The mixed group of adults who were working with children from 3-18 years created joint awareness of the restrictions placed on teachers of children in different age groups. The secondary level, multidisciplinary approach we created on those trips has now been seen to be a positive role model in the new Curriculum for Excellence in Scotland. The division of subjects goes against the idea of Malaguzzi's 'Hundred Languages of Children' as forms of expression of thinking. One occasion, when we were on the tiny rocky outcrop of Staffa, really stayed with me. All the scientific words and explanations could not define the feeling. The drum beat at the back of Fingal's cave, the fragility of the human voice against the power of the sea, experienced within something as awesome as the basaltic columns of the cave, silenced us all for some time. On return to the boat, people went into their own space to draw, write, play music, many just to be. Adults have become insular to the awe around them and the wildness in small spaces, but children have not. It took a large scale experience to reawaken the adult awareness. Children may feel that connectedness every day, and do we notice? Will we ever actually know? If we don't offer the opportunity, we can be certain it won't happen.

Let us look a little at how we access the experience of being in the 'wild'. The cognitive psychologists have explored the way that children think and learn. The image that we create a scaffold of known facts and then attach our new knowledge to it has been used for some time in education. They have referred to the process as 'inductive inference'. However, the new research suggests that perhaps we try to push children to think in an adult way. Inductive inference can be achieved in two main ways, category-based inference and similarity based inference. The category-based inference pulls information together and makes generalisations about the group in order to assimilate rapidly. Most adults seem to learn in this way until a 'specialist' develops. So we think of trees in a large group and make generalisations that there are deciduous and evergreen trees. In those groups we simplify the fact that evergreens are all conifers. In actual fact, not all conifers are evergreens. Adults appear to make assumptions that all the objects in the same group share all the same properties. This leads to inaccuracy.

Children, however, learn through similarity based inference where observations of similarities and differences lead children to create ideas such as frameworks of understanding. Each time a new piece of information comes along children look closely for similarities and differences. Looking at trees, they might create groups based on similarities such as bark that feels a certain way, trees that are by water, that have wobbly leaves, or branches with black buds. This way of looking at detail of similarities and differences is different to the way that most adults would look at them.

When we are working in the Nature Kindergartens, we consider the opportunities that children have to think about new information and give them the opportunity to look at similarities and differences of smaller groups to support their learning strategies.

I would say, the development of emotional resilience is cyclical. There is an inner strength that supports people in life to face some of the issues with a shield of resilience around them. The way that children develop this is through the development of the 'self'. It is extremely complex and we can only hope to start an awareness in this Chapter, however, since so much of what we do at Nature Kindergarten and Forest School is about 'self', then we should explore it in terms of its effect on learning.

Self-concept is our own perception of our unique personal characteristics such as appearance, ability, temperament, physique, attitude and beliefs. These determine our view of our place in society and our value in relationships. 'Self' concepts is therefore the umbrella term within which we find the various aspects of our ideas about self.

Self-image and the ideal self are connected in a relationship of variability. The two are connected since self-image represents 'who we are' and the ideal self represents 'where we would like to be'. Our self-image is created through the acquisition of perceptions of how we are accepted and valued. These relationships, at first with our parents and then with 'significant others', give us feedback that alters our perception of ourselves.

Ideal self is a mythical state that is created by our perceptions of the core features that people admire in us as individuals. When our relationships give us feedback that morals, respect, acceptable behaviour are valued, then we create an image of the aspiration of self.

Put simply, self-esteem is the relationship between self-image and the ideal self. If self-image is good and ideal self feels comfortably close then self-esteem is high and goals are seen as attainable and worth striving for. If self-esteem is poor and our ideal self seems out of reach, then our self-esteem will be low and efforts to improve will be regarded as temporary or ineffective.

Our children are treated as capable and that includes a joint understanding that they know what they are doing. Children are encouraged to experience the consequence of their actions, so children who choose to carry a log from the forest have to solve the way they will transport it. The perseverance with tasks over a number of weeks allows all children to achieve success through their own actions rather than through open-ended general praise. Children attend the nature kindergarten from 2 years old and seek 'attachment' to a parent/extended member of the family. For some children who already feel disequilibria between self and ideal self due to unrealistic expectations, we start with consistency and reliability across all areas of interaction, both inside and outside. This enables the adults to create a level of trust that can then go on to influence children's view of the adult opinion. To be a 'significant other' we need to earn the respect of the children in our care. The Rye philosophy, originally from Hungary has been very important in our work, long before we knew the word for it! Respectful care giving and working with children of all ages involves respecting that the time and action should be in the hands of the child. Our Nature Kindergarten staff strive to allow children to get themselves to somewhere when they are ready to do so, therefore feeling the relationship between cause and effect.

Case Study: 'Inside a Tree'

After a heavy snowstorm, many branches came down in our woodland including a very large branch of a Douglas Fir tree which had split into two. The space under the tree became the focal gathering place with children exploring the area in many different ways, some cutting and removing branches to add to their den, others climbing and hiding in the branches. One 3 year old boy lay on the branch looking up into the tall tree, while another pretended the tree was a space ship.

One 4 year old boy stroked the rough wood on the split branch, "This is the inside of the branch, where it tore off that tree up there…can you see right at the top where the white bit is, that's where it fell off". He sat on the branch and then slid into the split between the two halves, "I am inside the tree, this is like a squirrel inside his home in a tree and it used to be at the very top of the biggest tree and now it is down here!" For half an hour he lay there delighting in the

sense of being surrounded by the rough wood of the tree and finding himself in the middle of a part of nature which would normally be outside his reach.

Case Study: 'Tree Thinking'

Four 3 and 4 year old boys were sitting on a log in the woods looking around them and up into the trees where the leaves were starting to turn and fall off the trees. They talked about the shapes and colours of the leaves falling and commented that soon there would be no leaves left. One of them asked, "You know why the leaves are falling? The tree does not have enough water in it, in its roots, and the leaves go brown when they die and then they fall off". Looking at some fallen Sycamore leaves one commented, "Those black spots, the dots, those are where the leaves are sick but they still grow and fall off".

A 5 year old boy commented, "Christmas trees don't have leaves; they have needles but they are also leaves but just look like needles. Like Pine trees in the woods by the ponds. Evergreen, they are called evergreen because not all the leaves fall together in autumn so we can have a Christmas tree".

The discussion turned to animals that could be in the trees, "What do the squirrels do in autumn?" One asked, "they live high up in the trees. We need 'noculars' to see them". The boys selected binoculars from the Tree-Wrap™ which they had earlier stocked with resources they felt they would need in the woods.

The boys lay down in the damp grass and looked up into the trees. The talk continued, "Fairies live up there too, they help the animals get food, cause when it snows there is no food for animals in wintertime".

The children spotted a tiny mushroom growing under the tree and one observed, "Look, that's a fairy mushroom hiding from fox and people. That's the size of a fairy and they need it to fly to the top of the trees!" All four children then lay in comfortable silence looking up into the trees for a further 15 minutes. The image to the left took place back at the centre - the magical moment, a point in time out in nature was left as that, without analysis at the point. The reflection and revisiting took place later through a variety of different ways.

Key Points:

Learning is holistic; nature encourages cross curricular experiences.

The feedback and connection in a community of learning supports co-constructivism.

Nature offers 'magical moments' to deepen leaning in a way that is closely connected to the child.

Chapter 4

A place where adults and children enjoy each other's company

'Nature has given man one tongue, but two ears, that we may hear twice as much as we speak '.

Epictetus (Greek Philospher)

This chapter will explore some of the elements that we are currently exploring on the sites, that we feel are really important to the adult role in the Nature Kindergartens.

"Many adults talk about the joy of rediscovering 'how to learn' when they observe young children for the first time" (Lally, 1991). Adults who feel they are facilitators are more secure in the skill of standing back from the play in order to make sense of the action they see and to hear what young children are saying. They learn from the children, just as the children learn from the adults. This two-way dialogue enables the adult to match the level and type of provision to the types of frameworks and thoughts that the children are currently exploring and developing. One of the findings of the Effective Provision of Pre-School Education ('EPPE') project was linked to the degree of structure provided by an adult verses the autonomy of self directed play. The occurance of higher order thinking and levels of involvement were higher when there was a balance of support.

In the Nature Kindergartens we have tried to create an ethos of teachers as researchers so that we are constantly considering how we can improve our style of working. The centres are visited by thousands of people a year, who are looking for a more natural way to work with children, where ideas flow from the child and their voice can be heard from the forest through the Floorbooks and into daily planning. There is observation and assessment built in, in a way that is relevant and supportive of the child being a holistic learner. Tools such as FlipMino™ videos, sound recording materials and small note pads all fit into the hip belts that our staff use in the woods. Portfolios and learning stories are created through the year for adult reflection, children's voices are very prevalent throughout the process in the Talking and Thinking Floorbooks™.

The question of how to create a skilled workforce in early education is one that is on many agendas around the world. Looking at the content of the B.A in Childhood Studies currently being offered at some Scottish Universities, or the Early Years Practitioner qualification being developed across England, it is apparent that many of the skills of interaction and planning required for effective Nature Kindergarten practice are not developed in main stream courses. The Scottish plan to get everyone working towards a qualification and a graduate into every early years environment is offering many challenges from the small rural playgroup in the remote areas of Sutherland, right down to the large inner city spaces in Glasgow. Many wonderful 'educators' may be lost because of the need for paper evidence.

In actual fact, the aspects that we have been noting create the difference in the quality of staff and therefore in the provision, are more natural skills of human interaction that come from core being and are therefore difficult to teach.

- The ability to hold a conversation with a child because you really want to hear what he/she are saying.
- The ability to understand without having to always ask questions.
- An almost intuitive interpersonal intelligence which enables humans to 'read ' each other.
- The perseverance and enthusiasm to carry you, and the children near you, through the challenging weather days.
- The commitment and altruism to do what it takes.
- The knowledge to understand the journey of learning.

Skills and knowledge can be taught easily if the attitude and understanding are there. The term collegiality has come to represent the style of staffing we are encouraging at the kindergarten. The benefit of having people to work with children that have a life journey, gives the team a sense of balance, older members give a rooting, and people with diverse backgrounds give us the blend of skills that are important in our work. The blend of skills and talents is something that we have come to plan for. Our interview and selection process takes place in the forest.

Some of the staff may need to go on to gain more formal, or tailor made qualifications to look at methodology of working and playing outside, others have this approach hardwired so their training route will be into early education theories of learning.

Parents get involved in interviews as partners. Children's ideas are taken into account in that many ask for people with 'smiley faces, strong arms and hugs'. Alongside the coordinator of the centre sits an expert in more traditional outdoor education with a love of nature that has taken them to seek a qualification in Outdoor Education. We in turn support staff to gain the educational knowledge.

One of the aspects that has made itself very clear is that the learning is with the learner. Children learn very clearly, but have more retention when it is intrinsically motivated, when it inspires and connects to them. To understand these frameworks the adults are asked to do less talking and more listening.

Silence can teach through experience, is a wonderfully important statement. A neglected aspect of teaching is what I will term silence. It is however, far from that, there are many complex issues going on in silence. In actual fact many people see silence as a lack of something, whereas it is in fact hugely complex state of 'being'. Schwartz (1996), suggests that in view of its high symbolic and communicative importance, an interesting question is why silence does not feature more in academic writings on human communication and culture? One reason for this may be the 'slipperiness' of the concept, resisting definition and frequently used in a metaphoric rather than literal sense.

So, how can we define what we mean by 'silent pedagogy'? Ollin (2008), puts forward the idea that it is, "the complexity of the medium that has kept it in a secondary role to more overt pedagogical skills, in particular the skills involved in making conscious decisions not to initiate or intervene in particular classroom situations. Secondly, there are the ways in which learners interact or participate which are not manifested in talk or overt face to face engagement with others and which may be construed as passivity by observers in that they fail to conform to underlying preconceptions about the nature of participation and interaction".

The children at the Nature Kindergarten were watching a swan on the lake, the group had fallen silent. It would have been very inappropriate to break that connection to nature by asking questions such as, "what colour is that bird?" The process of being there and later drawing on your thinking to build a model, or reflect verbally on the experience, should be enough for us as evidence, if we really need that at all. The need for reciprocity is a pressure that children and adults feel when there is silence, the need to fill the gap, to make a joke, to ask a question are all techniques to deal with 'silence'. The complexity of the moment as Ollin suggests is often so very difficult to define. Multi layered complexity is in the mind of the learner, how do the adults begin to unravel all the concurrent thought processes. Even where the adult comes close to the learners moment, to transfer the ideas and concepts into a form that can be acknowledged and celebrated in a traditional view of 'education' in the UK is close to impossible, so we make choices about the elements to record, what to value and what to simply let go.

In silence the brain can process, reflect, consider, assimilate or discard ideas and then store pertinent information. I wonder how children find stillness and calm in some very large busy spaces. The fire circle is often quiet. The hammock area in the wood is often quiet. Children sit naturally at the base of trees, it doesn't mean that no learning is taking place.

The apprenticeship approach supports children to learn by being with groups of others who are older and younger than themselves. The family grouping can work very effectively as long as all the children are being challenged in their thinking. The positive effects of this approach have now influenced our connection to adults in the community. Children should be able to meet and learn from the community around them. An open play space in Denmark has pensioner housing in it's grounds – the oldest and youngest members of society share the same garden space. Each gaining from the presence of the other. That said, the wisdom of age is often not as celebrated in our western society as in many others. Time is a huge educator enabling us to experience moments that in turn, can influence the way we talk about issues with younger people. Having someone in your space to stimulate your ideas can happen in a non-verbal way. We have begun to ask visitors to come in to just 'be' in the space. The children are more natural in their interactions, engaging when they are ready. Enquiring and mimicking skills when interested. Too many visitors are placed on chairs and children are then faced with a strange stimulus for conversation. We would not do it with visitors to our house, so why do it in that way in an early learning environment?

Many people use the zone of proximal development put forward by Vygotsky's work to support the need for adult structure in learning through oral language and its connection to thinking. However, Vygotsky also referred to a process of maturation in which cognitive development is internalised, marked by a transition from vocalised cognitive processes to 'silent' inner speech, where thoughts remain private and vocalisation is a matter of personal choice. It is interesting that the pedagogical implications of these aspects of Vygotsky's work have been given far less attention than his ideas on the early relationship between thinking and vocalised language. The inner voice, the silence is as important as the overt systems of communication we put on children. In this sense, outdoor learning spaces that work in a natural way can afford as much learning as recorded learning outside or inside, we just need to 'trust' that it is happening and give them peace to think.

The connection between adults also becomes non verbal, in well skilled teams there is an automotive response so one is encouraged to settle and the other moves to have the overview of the space. The children feed off the emotion of this space since it is in a calm nurturing atmosphere with elements of activity, rather than always feeling that they have to race. Gentle interactions create an atmosphere of respect.

The presence of men on the team is worthy of mention since it does not happen regularly. Up to 50 per cent of the staff are male. When we asked them why early childhood here, their answer was because it works outside. Many indoor centres create an intuitive message of female dominance that cannot exist in the natural space. The outside area has no agenda and offers a very egalitarian space where all the adults within the space are real models of everything we have talked of. To sit silently in a state of presence, being mindful to the time and space you are in, is a wonderful gift for children. The affirming message that it is enough to 'be' in nature so that it nurtures us.

Case Study: 'The Woodworker'

Many skills that we use outside are different to those inside. Woodcarving and handling is one of the most wonderful ways to work with children. One of the parents came into the space at Whistlebrae to be with the children. The carving area was selected to be somewhere with little through traffic to give it a calmness. The area by the storytelling arbour was selected and the toadstool seats were used to sit on. The ceremony of preparation seems to engage children as tools appear and boundaries are arranged, there is already anticipation. The tools used for carving are very sharp and so the early explorations

happen with potato peelers to strip the bark, awls and the old drill bits are used to gauge out holes. The parent did not issue instructions or ask questions of the children. He calmly responded to any questions the children asked him and genuinely praised or advised on the work the children brought to him for comment. The children often work in this way in silence, sometimes chatting, often creating a social atmosphere, 'busy hands and a happy heart' as my mum used to say!

Case Study 'The Round House'

The projects can be small or large such as the creation of the wooden round house on the forest school site. The continuing spiral moves onwards in terms of complexity and challenge with children moving up this spiral at different rates and in slightly different helixes but all with the spiral. At the point in the forest where the round house was to go, the children explored the essence of the log, of a hole, of bark, of sawdust. Their understanding of the sustainability and respect for the forest and the wood it proferred was real.

The older children in the out-of-school care use the plane and spoke-shave to strip the bark from the sycamore and ash beams. They were harvested as part of the management of the forest and were therefore of low environmental impact'. The group of 8-11 year olds worked together to prepare the upright supports for the round house. The whole structure was made by hand - a

very real example of skilled craftsmanship by Chas and his team. The time it took allowed children to be involved in the reshaping of the landscape throughout. Holes were jumped in, materials collected for wooden sculptures to create a sculpture wall. Initial epistemic play moved on to be more transformational as the adults saw more imaginative representation taking place.

The skills displayed by the green woodworker were replicated in play. Children used bits of bark as spoke shaves; holes were dug and sticks erected in them in a variety of enclosure shapes; small round houses were built in ' communities' for the fairy folk; children chose to walk around with tool belts on and use 'their tools' to look at trees and judge their quality, speaking of straightness and height.

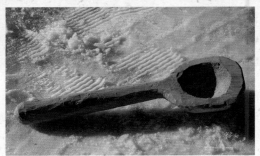

The stimulus of watching others around you is very powerful. If the task is smaller the effort involved is still as great for a child. Making mallets from wood in the forest allows each child to make their own and embellish the handle with colour and pattern (refer Journeys into Nature for detail).

There is progression in the type of tools used when the trust both within the group, and from the child to adult, increases. The spoon carving tools are used carefully and with care within the working area in the wild wood. The creation of spoons by the older children and their use, means there is a greater appreciation of the effort it takes to carve, sand and oil utensils. The care of the wooden bowls and spoons is very different from the metal spoons - both in the outdoor Kinder Kitchen and inside the camp area.

Children have the right to be in a place where adults enjoy being with them and treat them with respect. Giving time to build up relationships cannot ever be wasted, or less important, than external demands placed on childhood.

Key Points:

Collegiality provides a balanced, more natural way of adults and children being together.

Adult knowledge and skill supports effective interaction; not all effective interaction is verbal.

Relationships are at the heart of being human, so we should see family, community and the children within them as key aspects of our work.

Chapter 5

A place where there is a strong sense of family, community and fellowship

'Most people are on the world, not in it - having no conscious sympathy or relationship to anything about them - undiffused, separate, and rigidly alone like marbles of polished stone, touching but separate'.

John Muir

The word 'community' should be prevalent in early years work. Its meaning and relevance to educational policy in nations across the world, to regional areas and their implementation of the policy, to the people who live around an educational centre; the centre staff itself; the families that come to it and then of course to the most important element, the children themselves.

Let us start this chapter by starting at the outer most ring of the sense of community and gradually consider how we work to the child themself.

Community of nations

The range of climatic regions that we inhabit affects the way nature looks in nations around the world. From arctic tundra to hot desserts, children will be playing outside.

Nations have a cultural heritage that affects their connection to nature. There are some peoples who have really developed a 'sense' of nature because their path is inextricably linked to it either in history or currently. The Celts of Scotland who lived in Crannogs, Aboriginals and Torres Strait Islanders, First Nation peoples, people of remote parts of Nepal for example, in fact one could say that anyone who has to connect to nature in order to survive, has to have a tradition of connection and a knowledge of the space they are in to create intergenerational knowledge. Yet the endurance of intergenerational knowledge fascinates me. The knowledge that we need now to help us live sustainable lives was there all that time ago. Why do most people in the nominally called 'developed' world consider it to be less vital to us than a laptop? One magnetic surge and they would all stop and all the computerised systems would grind to a halt. The sustainability of the globe is in the focal point now, but it is becoming critical. In November 2009 the largest iceberg calved from the arctic ice shelf. We need to look at a shared earth, rather than a processed one. One wonders who has evolved!

Nations have created a place for nature in their policies, but the way in which it is threaded through all aspects, or sits merely in one location, albeit a small location in some cases, is truly challenging. The Nature Action Collaborative for Children (NACC), of which we are a part, is designed to create a professional group of people to create a network of support around the globe so that Irma in Swaziland can work alongside Wil in Belize to challenge national communities to take notice.

Some people, choose a single path in their work to challenge governments. A single voice can create a ripple, which in turn affects someone else and so the effect widens. The desire to define our approach to Nature Kindergarten has come from a desire to protect something rather than the concept be watered down to be little more than playing outside. It is not a walk, nor a visit to a park, it is far more and through the creation of the Mindstretchers' Nature Kindergarten, as a defined approach, we hope to support people across the world to create something with similar values to those laid out in this book. Through this type of vision people can start to have conversations, they can make connections and applications to their own climatic area. To support Bush Schools in Australia, to inspire the development of Nature Kindergartens in New Zealand, and to see their rise in the United Kingdom has been a delight. There will always be interagency politics and ego centric people who can actually divide, but as long as there are enough people who believe in collegiality then the change process will carry on.

The travelling that I do to lecture and share the approach, has shown me many things. The common bonds and links around the world has to be the greatest. To meet Anders in Norway and then Bishnu in Nepal, Toni and Robyn Christie in New Zealand along with many others , is very affirming - we are all moving in a similar direction. All different pathways, but leading to the same place like the tributaries on a river system, when we all join together the effect is so much more powerful.

The Norwegian approach was beautifully shared by Anders Farstad at an outdoor conference with us in Scotland. In his kindergarten, young children are outside or sitting on reindeer hides around an open fire in a small log cabin. They are encouraged to charge about, climb trees, they learn how to use tools, including axes to chop wood, and they light fires and cook fresh food over them – often the fish they caught whilst out fishing in the kindergarten's own fishing boat. As I touched upon earlier, there is in Norway a long tradition of nature as a place for recreation.

Being close to the natural elements is highly valued. There is a pedagogic view that nature gives children a lot of freedom. There are no walls or regulations to shut us in. So the children don't have to shout or fight to gain a bit of space or attention from the grown-ups.'

Community of culture

To take this methodology and put it into another culture without adaptation would be inappropriate, to take the elements and values, to be mindful as to what they mean to the people in the community, to be discursive and considered, will create a close link. The world is very diverse and cultural beliefs do not link to one physical country or to a nation. The example of the Italian approach to cold weather is still present today, the idea that it will make you sick pervades! If the culture is that you do not play in dirt then there are multiple barriers to challenge no matter what country you live in. Raed in Jordan is a colleague from the NACC and he is moving forward the culture of those around him in Jordan, to look at the earth as a positive thing to play with.

Community of location

The smaller location of the inner community of a smaller geographical area brings us in to the smaller differences in attitude to outdoor connection perhaps between communities in a city, or between an urban and a rural location. There are reasons why adults gravitate to different spaces, some of it is environmental experience, or it is just the simple choices that life offers. Everyone needs try to be open to the possibility that all humans have a connection or even an awareness of the effect of nature. As I aimed to illustrate above, the local parent community should be an intrinsic part of any centre - their beliefs and visions for their own children is of course central to our joint care approach. Local communities will be involved in their local environments, whether they connect to the natural beauty of the space (urban and rural alike), or see it as just a location is the question. There are wonderful examples where the children

have brought together community. I am thinking about the reclamation of abandoned woodlands and the intergenerational conversations to discover older traditional remedies and tips for using nature's harvest, or to share stories of risk full days and long hot summers in Scotland.

Community with 'local people'

The young children in the kindergarten have the opportunity to share 'local place based knowledge' with the adults around them. Listening to the children brings a clear message of their engagement and enjoyment of the process orientated work. Their faces as we make bread together, as fruit they have picked is used for the daily food is wonderful. My earlier book Journeys into Nature was created to reflect natural ways of being. There is a loss of the most traditional skills of preserving jam, drying fruit, building clay huts and weaving mats. The sustainable traditions are important to the human race, because they do reconnect us to the natural world, when we see it in the role of provider. When we lose that accumulated information, and skill level, it will take many years to develop again. The apparently simplest of experiences can have the most complex learning. The collection of brambles in Scotland will have the same affect on individual emotions as blueberries in America, or harvesting an aubergine in Italy.

In 2008, I was exploring the possibilities of supporting the development of Bush Schools in Australia and what similarities and connection would be climatically, culturally and community relevant. Nev and I went into the bush and as I shared, so he shared, showing me an Australian equivalent. Plant dyes, shelter types, ochre from the earth, tinder for a fire from inside a plant, Grass Tree gum and kangaroo dung as a resin to make an axe, there were so many links that we could have walked for a long time. Nev felt that it was vital that children listen to the land and become connected to it, it was astonishing for me that this group of people were only really acknowledged by others in the 1960's. In 2009 on return, I was lucky enough to have a special invitation to spend some time at a centre in Tamworth, inland of Sydney, where their journey into nature was really just beginning. The staff especially the cook had a strong affinity to the sense of place that I shared with her, a reflective process that will hopefully support the adults to look to their own intergenerational knowledge to create a natural playspace that celebrates their sense of place as it is now and what it has been.

Bronfenbrenner (1990), describes the child's expanding world, developing from a secure base to explore similarities and differences that connect them to, and distinguish them from others. Humans link to each other through commonality of experience, recipes are often a topic of conversation when we first work with groups, shared understanding of a 'good one' even down to the method of making petal perfume, or rose petal paper. With a positive self image, the child is likely to treat cultures and beliefs of others with respect. One way to increase that self-image is to enable there to be a feedback loop of success, what better way to start this aspect than through a global recipe book for bread.

The sense of belonging that comes from preparing and cooking together has long been noticed by team development analysts. The children enjoy the process, parents come in to share their version of a flat unleavened bread from chapatis, to tortilla to damper. A global network of similarity that children can feel very much involved with.

Community of the centre

Importance of collegiality cannot be stressed enough. The staff, parents and children all create a community. The form it takes will and should vary across the globe, because the early year's provision sits firmly in the community. The culture and ethos of institutions and wider culture of the societal norms will affect the perception of the provision. Within the space that the children come to there is a sense of community. It is created through many things including shared thinking and understanding, an ethos of trust, importance of family, a nurturing space. The journey to create a nature kindergarten is as much about the minds of the people as it is about the landscape.

Community of 'I, you and us'

Is the place of real community actually in the distance between two individuals? The movement from casual friendship to the place of an intuitive understanding is also referred to as community in mentoring teams. People who have experienced a joint 'magical moment' as adults in nature will know what I mean by that sense of community. It carries on in a way far beyond the actual experience. Children may feel this and not be able to vocalise it, in the very least we can hope that the experiences we offer at the kindergartens will set them on a journey, whereby they may get there one day in the future. The feeling described by us was a sense of bonding. Joseph Clinton Pearce (1977), uses this term to look at the way that children bond to nature through moments that may disappear over time. I would consider that children are so closely connected to nature that they are also part of this bonding process. Feeling that you are valued as an individual within a larger framework of community is what gives us a sense of self.

I keep coming back to this point, because it is so vital - the parents are an integral part of what we do at the Nature Kindergartens. They have a group that has become an entity in itself of people coming together to meet and talk, to work within the woods and also to meet as families to support each other. The link for children between a familiar home space and their place of care creates security; the adults around them talking, laughing, connecting is an affirmation for many that they are in a place of stability. Seeing the people around you link, creates a complete picture, a frame for the young child that gives them a sense of where they are, who they are and where they can 'belong'.

Chapter 6
A place that gives a sense of belonging

'A smile is the light in the window of your face that tells people you're at home'.

Anonymous

Nature is so varied in all its forms that to simply restrict children's experience to one particular space or type of wild space would be to lose the variety of life. The sense of place that children have is the link between themselves, their immediate culture and the way that the community interrelates to the wider environment. A child's sense of place is an internal anchor that provides a sense of belonging. Maudsley (2005), provides an outline that covers all aspects of encounter so that a wild space or a natural space simply becomes somewhere where nature has the upper hand! The places may be completely natural, such as ancient woodland or be mixed in with a few manmade artificial elements, such as in adventure playgrounds or urban parks. So, what are these varied forms? Wild spaces come in many different shapes and sizes, and can be large or small, wet or dry, open or enclosed, near or far, tall or short, messy or tidy, green or brown. Wild spaces include country lanes, hedgerows, woodland, city farms, grassland, beaches, heathland, gardens, rivers, shrubs, verges, ponds, fields, hills, parks, trees farmland, sand dunes, village greens and muddy hollows. The way that children access all of these areas depends of course, amongst other reasons, on the location. The point is that we should not narrow our thinking to Nature Kindergartens since that is only one form of habitat.

Robert McFarlane (2007), suggests through his journeys in search of wild spaces that in fact, 'wildness' exists in the micro scale in a square of grass, at the root of a tree and certainly not only at the top of an exposed mountainous ridge where we might traditionally consider the wilderness to be.

There is a fundamental aspect of our human existence that must go back to the times when our ancestors created a place to enclose us but also to be able to look out, to peep, to assess what is going on outside the space we are in. So, it is with children and their families when we go into nature. Almost all the people that we have worked with have remembered a den from their childhood, often kept secret from adults - a space where they had ownership. The sense of shelter is very powerful especially when it is transferred to a wild space. When

nature provides the building materials, it is as if everything has a purpose and reason. The branches fall, they are used by flora and fauna (which includes us), and then they return to the earth from whence they came. The cycle works, it is only when we over design it that it becomes interrupted and disjointed. When engaged in activities in natural settings, such as den building, collecting objects and exploring routes, children are responding to evolutionary psychological desires to connect with place and natural landscapes (Herrwagen and Oriens, 2002).

The issue in many centres today is that over designed materials such as pop up tents have taken away some of the thinking, designing, problem solving skills and most importantly, the affirmation for children of having created something unique.

The loose materials for making dens need to be available. In some spaces, we provide a variety of materials of different types and properties so that real choices are being made. In the Nature Kindergartens the materials come from nature. The woodland is left to provide natural hiding

holes created by the trees; children work within a landscape, changing altering it and in some cases having to adjust their thinking to meet the unyielding aspects of the landscape they are working within.

Some of the children created a den 'below' rather than a den elevated up, which is often the traditional way to look at dens. They learned about support structures and digging down to reinforce the sides and the entrance. The secret world of underground has often been used as a focus to create a tunnel in a visitor centre. This is great, as long as the architects do not overlook the core experience of smell. The earth has a wonderful smell that although not bottled and sold in perfume shops, is as evocative as cut grass.

Low level shapes curved out of the ground do have a wonderful solid feel that can give feelings of enclosure that would be hard to obtain in an elevated den. In the Waldkindergarten near Nurnburg in Germany, there were 6/7 children playing as a group. The gathering space in the forest as I mentioned in Chapter 3, was a large circular dip in the ground. The space provided enclosure and some shelter from the wind, there was another tarpaulin shelter about a 100 yards away. Children lay along the rim, vertically down to the base of the hollow, curled at the bottom of the hollow. A tree sapling created the bouncing experience and the old stronger trees created the back rest for the semi-recumbent. The children were also engaged in very different experiences from gazing up into the trees, to carving, to bouncing, to talking, all joined together in different moments and then moving in and out of the group dynamic whilst still being physically close. The dip provided a point of focus; the space could easily have been a giant log or a leaf bower. In this space, at this time, it was a dip.

People mark their space, they make a totem, or a marker such as a stone in a forked branch to say that they are here, or have been here. If we consider the cave paintings and markings of early settlers, they were positioned in places that mattered to them. Often near natural shelters they created an image, a representation of their own human embodiment. We have observed children create crosses, a line of pebbles, a stone in a forked stick with no formal instruction or indeed awareness of all the tradition that sits with the human race behind them.

The boundaries are more fully explored in the chapter on transitions, but let us just note here that the entrance point from one space to another is a rite of passage, a presence of mind that defines that sense of place.

Chawla (2002), suggests that playfully investing cultural meaning and

mythic significance onto natural spaces and features occurs with far more frequency than in fabricated play spaces. The natural spaces offer a stimulus that goes beyond sheer materials into something more emotive and personal.

A group of children created a woodland elf, or gatekeeper at the junction of two paths to mark their presence in the space. A group of students visiting us from Nova Scotia talked of their version of this called the 'Inukshuk'. Due to the nature of their natural landscape the material used is stone. This stone figure is often depicted in Canadian art. It has arms made of one long slab of stone that point along a path to safeguard travellers.

If we look to the tradition of cairns, they are not only for way marking in bad weather but also to mark the passage of the walker. It is often an automatic gesture on top of a mountain or moor to put a fragment on the cairn, just to say in a small way that a human was here in this vastness. Vastness or wildness for a 4 year old can be in a small area of long grass. Perhaps wildness is a space or place in the mind evoked by the landscape around us. Does it need to be vast, to be inaccessible or can we find wildness in smaller spaces closer to home?

There have been many times where the staff team working in the woods or out in nature have discussed how long natural structures should be left up. The sense of place suggests an essence of permanence and yet we have explored the opposite in terms of landscape. It is the moving through that connects humans everywhere and so it is that we now look at object permanence.

We have explored the way that children's play evolves, the decision of how and when the decision should be left to the children. There are a number of dens on the woodland site, which are left and then revisited over time. We have been unable to ascertain why a particular den is seen to be the one for 'this time'. There is no pattern linked to weather, or key dominant children. When we asked the children to share their decision making, they merely replied 'well because it is'. Empirical research into this feature would be fascinating, enlightening.

The same approach has led us to consider all aspects of our provision. We now allow nature to reclaim back the logs from a homemade xylophone, the string and the den roofs on the forest site. The adult perceptions have moved on to see the areas of abandonment not as untidy piles

but as spaces that provocate thinking and offer opportunities for reflection. In the garden spaces, natural objects are left if they do not impact on too much visual clutter, they offer special moments with frogs nestling in children's miniature dens and slugs taking up the form of the carved shapes in soft wood. Conversations have become richer, deeper and more perceptive about why things need to go back to the earth. "If you keep taking it out (the timber),... well it (the earth), will get exhausted and then it won't be able to make any more, it needs us to share and give it back". If only this 4 year old had the chance to raise questions about sustainability with policy makers and global leaders.

Case Study: 'Children as Designers'

The creation of structures and its link to a sense of place was explored when the geodome sheet at Whistlebrae had to be removed for cleaning. We had seen the geodome as a shelter, but from the children's perspective it was clear that it marked their space. This thinking was extended through the creation of new panels made by children to replace the canvas and actually created something far richer.

Outdoor spaces in the U.K. need to provide some form of base to create shelter for young children. The shelter can offer wonderful opportunities for learning and exploration if the children are encouraged to be integral to the ideas. One of the forms of shelter in our woodlands are canvas geodomes and during a discussion about removing the canopy for cleaning, the children noted that the frame consisted of triangles. They suggested decorating the triangles and drew their designs, "That's the geodome getting taken off"; "Geodome, it lives in the wood!"

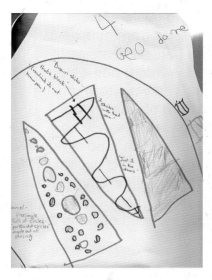

"One triangle full of circles - polka dot circles made out of string!" "The grey bits are windows from plastic!"

"My window has wool like worms". "Mine makes the trees blue...look".

The essence of triangularity and the way that shapes tessellate became the focus for the focus area. The use of 2d and 3d materials allows children to choose the way that they present their thinking. The documentation and consultation that runs throughout this process is a very significant part of the approach. To consult children and then not act upon those decisions is false and will not lead to a sense of belonging. The use of digital technology allowed plans to be photocopied and used many times to add new patterns and ideas, cameras were used to record their models and draft ideas allowing the staff to document the process of exploration that ultimately lead to the laminated panels seen on page 51.

To extend the experience children were supported in the indoor space with a provocation board which included child and adult drawings, photographs and materials such as twine, sticks, tape, wire, cellophane and paper.

They then created the miniature panels using a variety of materials. Children went on to create fairy geodomes and then their own mini geodome using triangles they made of sycamore sticks and wire. "That's me doing the weaving in the triangles". "I tied stuff, just bits and bobs".

The way into naturalistic spaces has also evoked real feelings of place and ownership. It is a common experience across centres that the children design their boundaries from outside to inside. Some children transfer issues of security to this type of play and bring in locking mechanisms, burglar alarms, pits and other traps. One boy created a stone door bell which changed it's tune according to the position of the stone in the cleft stick. The wait from ringing the doorbell stone and letting you in was indicative of the child's experience of waiting for visitors to climb the stairs up to his flat. The territory created by the enclosure of space so that it becomes 'my place' is something of note within the play behaviours. At what point does the sense of place become mine and therefore exclusive of others. Case studies collected over time have shown that children use traditional role play areas for a social hierarchy and sometimes exclusion. The relocation outside to the wild wood saw the play behaviours change from exclusive to inclusive. The question about space as a factor, or open ended designs that created more socialisation is as yet undecided.

Nabhan and Trimble (1994), relate how finding, playing with and taking home natural loose objects, 'treasure' transfers the uniqueness of the possession onto the child – 'this stick is special, and so am I'. There are times when children have collected materials from the wood and are desperate to take the materials home. The transference suggested by Nabhan and Trimble from natures treasure to the self is of note, and yet so is the environmental impact of the removal of natural habitats on a daily basis. The work we do has suggested virtual photos, real photos, special placing of key objects and the celebration of departure so that the reconnection can happen the next day. Only a few children actually sustain the connection from day to day, they are usually engrossed in the search for objects, unless of course it is a prize stick!

The connection to nature is intuitive rather than cognitive and so is often hard to articulate. The presence of a group that creates community within a space; a repeated visit to the same space; a sense of guardianship and connection of the natural environment work; a place that has a connection to your deep rooted thinking and culture that reflects the background of the family will all anchor children.

Key Points:

Young children have a natural connection to nature that connects them to a space that they visit and get to know.

Play is often more transformational in the wild woods and moves more frequently than in the garden area.

A sense of belonging is important for children, especially in the 'wildness' of nature.

Chapter 7

A place of trust and democracy

'You can't be suspicious of a tree, or accuse a bird or a squirrel of subversion or challenge the ideology of a violet. The human spirit needs places where nature has not been rearranged by the hand of man'.

Hal Borland, et al.

The creation of a culture of democracy is a subtle procedure that takes place over years. The value that we as humans place on ideas that children have, the status that they have in the actions we take should be high. The use of documentation processes are not enough in themselves, the way that the documentation is used and applied is the step that leads us to a democratic culture with classrooms and communities of learning.

The emphasis is not on children as the sole leaders but an equilibrium balance - multiple minds negotiating, being mindful of others. All humans need to feel as if they are valued and that the person they are talking with will be an active listener. The development of trust works at a deep level. It is a blend of emotional connections over time and experiences, that the others around you will do as they say, take actions and accept their part in the community of learning.

Decision making can be autocratic or democratic. Some decisions are made by an adult to set boundaries, to reinforce expectation, to analyse learning and proffer a next step. The democratic element of early years development can be misinterpreted as a 'free for all'. In actual fact it is a much more subtle process of calm assertiveness and expectation that develops a relaxed harmonious group that feels secure within the boundaries created.

The exploration of the wild space at Kindergarten and Forest School requires group working, a joint understanding of the expectations of behaviour. A visual boundary is up around both wild spaces that is created and reinforced by staff and children together. This joint responsibility is another aspect that leads to a democratic way of working. If the boundaries are crossed or the group do not work together then there will be 'meeting'. Meetings are not the same as group time as they are called by children or adults, the subjects that they wish to talk about vary from day to day. We have had in depth moments about how to keep the moss safe after it started to disappear from the trees. Children have called meetings about the amount of raisins they want to eat at 'snack'. The minutes of the meetings and the decisions made are noted. This record goes into the Floorbooks so that they can be referred back to at any point. The older the children, the more they use the minutes of the meetings to assert their view.

Trust is a massive part of what we are trying to create at the Nature Kindergarten and Forest School. It is a slow process and for some children on the Forest School programme for 5-11 years, the weekly three hour session is only a superficial amount that can start to show an alternative vision or possible pathway for children. If the experience at home has been inconsistent, children begin to mistrust adults across all aspects of their education and care. The adults at the site have been supported to create SMART targets - small, achievable, relevant targets to ensure that children feel the feedback loop of personal achievement.

The outdoor environment has been used by adults as a place to develop 'trust', suspended by a rope, you need to rely on the person holding onto the other end. Children feel the same level of emotion when they go onto a log, or use a rope to climb over a boulder, that they could easily do without the assistance of an adult. There must be some enjoyment of physically being connected to another, because all children seem to seek out rope to hold onto, to tie themselves together, or to lay on the ground to enclose themselves and their friends as a form of security.

In the Waldkindergarten there was a real development of trust, in that older children were allowed to travel on in front of the main walking group, cross a track and enter the building the group were using for lunch. The forest is a public space and held fears for the staff, that prevented the children's freedom and automony.

We are working to develop our sense of location so that we can allow children some freedom to move at their pace when they are on the walk between clearings. The benefit risk assessment is such that the children do not have the degree of freedom in the vicinity of deep water. We do however, encourage it in the 'dry wood' where they go on ahead to locate at 'meeting trees'. The trees and locations are of note in themselves since they have attracted children's attention through their position, beauty or abnormalities that make them unique in the wood. In a woodland in Germany, the children talked of the 'Lion Tree'. It had been noticed by children many years ago and so now the mark is two metres up. The children spoke of it with a sense of tradition, a place where children had been there before, their own parents perhaps? A simple mark on the tree gave the area a sense of gravitas, an anchor to the past. I'll talk more about this tree in Chapter 11.

The freedom we want children to have will retain the childhood memories so many of us had. In order for the adults to scaffold this we need to re-assert the values of the approach in that every child is competent, that they can be trusted if we build up a relationship.

The control of being out of control, having the confidence to let go, is a very important emotional skill. Whistlebrae has a slope to the forest floor - it takes effort to climb up and confidence to run down. Do I trust that the children will

not keep on running out of the forest and down the road as in the film of Forest Gump? Yes, I do. Part of that is an inner confidence of the adult and some linked to the knowledge of the children you work with. For the groups that are connected to the centre such as registration bodies, visitors and onlookers, they do have the background of the effectiveness of staff relationship with a group of children.

Some groups can find it very hard to assess trust on a short visit to the wild woods, so the adults put procedures in place. The adults want to preserve the right to run down a slope, so they have a meeting place at the top and one at the bottom underneath the most awe inspiring rhododendron tree. Ironically, the procedure is there to ensure that the freedom continues in childhood.

The experience and connection to strategies used by outdoor educators that we have seen in Germany and Denmark was affirming for us as a team.

It has started to influence the content of a pedagogue based qualification for outdoor learning that contains skills appropriate to being part of a multidisciplinary team of outdoor pedagogues.

The children have a sense of trust that if they need something they will get it. Not a resource necessarily but a greater connection, an affirmation, time perhaps. Agendas for outdoor learning environments have to be flexible. The landscape changes every day, every hour in fact and every minute. Light creates a mood in a wild space. It is it's very attraction and strength. This very changeability is the element that engages us all, keeping the brain engaged and fully stimulated if we have the eyes to notice it all. When children find a hole, it can be explored for as long as it takes, giving children time to revisit it to be mindful of how it alters with light, temperature, moisture; the flora and flora around it. There were a number of children in the Waldkindergarten who found a clay shallow. The temperature had been well below freezing so that the water had partly frozen the mud to change its texture. Children automatically de-construct to re-construct, so they tried to break the surface ice.

Children need to feel trust on a number of different levels; as learners, risk takers and explorers. The ethos brings with it an educational standpoint. What is our educational system trying to support? Divergent or convergent thinkers? People who use possibility thinking or thinking about conformity?

Case Study: 'Frozen Bandages'

In Germany a group of children were sitting next to a frozen puddle in the woodland moving leaves around with sticks or their fingers as they talked. The adults were in a different part of the woodland site and not within earshot. There is a trust between the adults and the children that allows adults to feel that they do not need to be in close proximity to the children for engaging play and learning to take place. One 4 year old girl discovered a patch of sandy mud where the ice had melted.

She stirred it with her stick and then rubbed the sand between her fingers before scooping up a handfull and forming it into a small ball. The conversation changed and the group moved closer together to share this experience and collect more mud by enlarging the mud hole. They spent some time manipulating the sandy mud between their fingers and creating balls until the little girl pushed her thumb through the ball of mud and showed the others "plaster, look I made a plaster to fix my sore finger." The whole group then created mud bandages to cover imaginary wounds by either pushing their finger through a ball of mud or manipulating the mud around their fingers. The conversation turned to how they had sustained the injury, the size of injury and bandage and the length of time they would need to recover. A 5 year old boy told the group

that he had once broken his arm, the bandage they put on had to be very hard and he could not bend his arm. "We can freeze the bandage to make it hard", "That would be very cold", "Maybe cook it like bread? Mmm…but not when it is on". "Dry mud is hard so you can sit very still until it is dry and then it is hard". With this solution the group then sought out the adults to share this information with them.

The children were allowed and empowered to choose to keep the mud for some time to feel and see the changes in temperature adhesion and appearance. The adult interaction should be one of real interest to co-construct new understanding for all involved.

Key Points:

Communities develop trust through long term consistent relationships.

Democratic learning environments have to be built on trust.

Autonomy in thinking will support a co-constructivist model of teaching and learning that in turn, supports divergent thinking.

Chapter 8
A place where you are consulted

'It comes down to voices enabling choices'

Claire Warden

Creating a stimulating place for children to be cared for now carries with it the need to demonstrate quality. This in itself is good, I agree that we need to make sure that children have high quality care. The down side to this development has been people's perceptions of what quality is, what it looks like. The Nature Kindergartens are rich in terms of relationship, community and the land around them, but to some the reuse of materials, being in mud and having to gather creative materials from the wild is seen to be the poor side of the fence. Yet when we observe children, their bodies show us that they want to dance in leaves, to pick them up and explore all their potential. Their voices tell us that making a spy hole in the leaf is the most wonderful experience, that it made their day 'the best ever'. Interestingly, the next day will be even better, because as a team we will attempt to create a synergy between the child and the space. Our role is to do this through the Talking and Thinking Floorbooks™, our consultative approach to the journey of assessment and planning. When I developed the approach in the1980's, it was in an attempt to engage a group of boys in the learning process through greater empowerment. Clark, McQuail and Moss (2003), have gone on to identify how rarely children are consulted about their own education, still less about their own educational success. Consultation with children is important because:

• It creates a closer match between the child and the curriculum being experienced.
• It builds self esteem and positive attitudes when the learner is involved in the decision making.
• It increases intrinsic motivation that stays with a child throughout life.
• Children have a right to be treated with respect as individuals. We can show respect by valuing their thoughts and opinions.

There are key features of a Talking and Thinking Floorbook™ that can create a more effective tool for assessment, planning and ultimately a community of learning.

Children's ideas and thoughts are put into the book without re-framing or interpretation so that they are a genuine record of their thinking. When children give a response to a question or contribute an idea that is far removed from the rest of the group thinking, the idea should be recorded as evidence of contribution, but not necessarily of engagement with the subject.

Open ended questions are created in response to an interest from the children. The questions are posed as part of a conversation and are designed to stimulate thought rather than test knowledge. The flow of reflective talk is critical to the process, to create a partnership of exploration and discovery. Question and answer sessions create a completely different atmosphere. Any questioning used are almost philosophical, such as I wonder what would happen if..?

The objective is to encourage divergent thinking, that encourages higher order thinking. Challenging children to create links in their own learning can stimulate this level of interest. Revisiting ideas over long blocks of time support children to see that the process of thinking and learning is full of experimentation and adaptation. This process of metacognition is very important to the assimilation of concept, knowledge or attitude.

The flow of the Floorbook follows children's desires to explore an area in depth. Depth of learning created through giving children time to explore their own thinking is the key to long term embedded knowledge. Collating children's ideas in a book form ensures that the group focus on continuity and progression over longer blocks of time. There should be a link between pages and a flow through the book so the journey is a series of linked steps.

Some of the children at the Kindergarten attend for shorter sessions over the week. These children need support to pick up the threads. Where are we now? What have we discovered since you were last here? How shall we go forward from here? Are all questions that the children can discuss in pairs or small groups when they have a Floorbook to look at as a memory prompt.

The books include very large pieces of blank paper that enable children and adults to record their ideas as a group - collaborative learning. By giving each person a different coloured marker it is possible to observe who contributes to the group writing. The adult provides a role model for the process of thinking, listening, supporting, suggesting ideas, accepting challenge, of being a writer, making of diagrams, Mind Maps™ to name just a few.

The requirements for accountability have lead to a requirement for daily planning. These books are cross referenced to the plans so that the child's thought, and the adult's response and then an action are all linked and can be tracked through dated entries, together with an overview to monitor breadth and balance.

To respond to different learning styles and preferences, the Floorbooks incorporate a wide genre of writing. The adult can scribe for the children to release some of the pressure of secretarial skills during a small group experience; individuals can record their idea in a pictorial form, or writing on a thinking bubble. We have a thinking tree outside that has a place as a location to sit and ponder, but also as the location for the outdoor session.

Talking and Thinking™ Floorbooks are an integral part of our planning. They are created with children during the play session, and are used to analyse the starting points for learning that children are suggesting, rather than adults thinking up random 'activities' for children to 'do'. Responsive planning should be at the root of learning. If we are going to consult children then we should be prepared to change our thinking and actions as a result of it. The books are available to children at all times. Joint ownership should give children the right to revisit their thinking whenever they wish. There has to be a feedback loop to the children so that they know that the process of consultation is actually changing something.

In practice, this approach has led to a child centred curriculum, that is based on evidence collated in a child centred way. A feature that many centres felt is being edged out by paperwork demands.

The children drive the content of the Floorbooks and as a mentoring vehicle they make the action behind the planning very visible. The purposeful contexts the children bring forward are things such as mud, a slope, ice, a leaf, fire but the learning inside is wide and often the thread of the book cannot be defined until the journey is well underway. The floorbooks are integral to our work since they are the root of empowerment and democracy.

Case study: 'Butterflies'

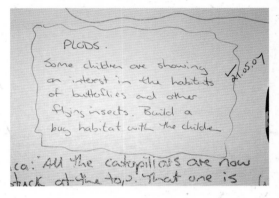

A 3 year old girl was creating her representation of a butterfly and asked the group, "How many legs butterflies got?" A 5 year old boy replied, "Butterflies don't have legs!" The adult felt that an in depth investigation into butterflies would be a P.L.O.D. (Possible Line Of Development) allowing children to explore the structure and life cycle of butterflies.

Caterpillars were ordered, arrived in a tub with a food medium and children could closely watch the growth of the caterpillars, "They are growing, they are bigger and eating the food", "I can see they have spikes", "They live in there? They not coming out?" A P.L.O.D. from this comment was to investigate bug habitats.

"All the caterpillars are now stuck at the top. That one has changed into a cocoon!", "Those are going to turn into 'flutterflies', fish are going to turn into ....fish!" One 4 year old girl commented on the silk thread connecting the cocoon, "That's the swing when they turn into a butterfly". Using the identification charts, awareness was raised about different species of local butterflies, as well as those from other countries and the adult provided images of an assortment of exotic butterflies. When the butterflies hatched the children spent time caring, observing, discussing and drawing the features that most interested them, the wings, the legs and the curly tongue.

One butterfly died and children examined it under the digital microscope. "I didn't know butterflies had hair, I can see hair on its body!", "Two big eyes and look, I can see a curly tongue", "I can see it has

feets". The P.L.O.D. was to look at other insects and bugs under the microscope to compare features and classify them. While using the microscope and moving the butterfly with a finger a 4 year boy commented, "Look, that is my finger! I can see my nail, it is long. I am moving it, look, look it is huge – a giant finger!" The P.L.O.D. took children on a side journey looking at other human features for a short while and then returned to butterflies.

At the end of the investigation the adult was able to collate a summative assessment of children's knowledge by providing a Talking and Thinking Tree™ surrounded by visual provocations of butterflies for children to share what they knew about butterflies.

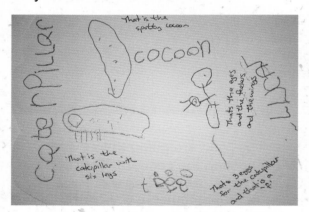

The language of that reflection was of the children; the 'squidginess' of caterpillars, 'tickliness'of butterflies were all accepted and valued as key knowledge.

Children have key pieces of knowledge, attitudes and concepts that have been gathered over their short but dynamic life. They apply these frameworks so well that they almost go unnoticed, until someone gives them the time to speak and be listened to in the bustle of the process of life.

Key Points:

The learning process is more effective when children are consulted about their understanding and own next steps.

The floorbooks show group progression, along lines of enquiry that are often very closely aligned to nature.

Learning is within a community of learning. Small family groups support a more natural way to learn.

Individual learning stories create effective personal reflection records.

Chapter 9

A place to work in harmony with nature

'Some of nature's most exquisite handywork is on a miniature scale as anyone knows who has applied a magnifying glass to a snowflake'.

Rachel Carson

In days gone by there was a real connection to the cycle of the year. Wherever you are on the globe there will be something that heralds the passage of a point of change. For example, a clearly visible seasonal change, such as weather is a different point for discussion. If we look at the detail of change, say, the cycle of reproduction in plants and animals we need to explore subtle changes. In the UK we have four seasons. My colleague from Perth in Australia who I talked about earlier, used a wallaby skin to re-awaken the awareness of the six seasons or states that indigenous peoples have an awareness of.

A beautiful book called D'harawal (Bodkin 2008), compiled by a group from Sydney explores a multilayer approach to understanding change. Their close connection to the earth enabled them to see and feel the most subtle of changes that to most people would all be grouped under a general statement of 'its hot'! Their knowledge base has been created over such a long period of time that they have had to work in harmony with nature in order to survive. It is wonderful to see an acknowledgement of this community knowledge so that following generations continue to learn from it.

A large part of what we do reconnects children to a way we can work in harmony with nature, and in that way it sustains us. Healthy, additive free food is a core need for children and it features very highly in our work. Children make bread every day. Yeast based recipes are made in the bread maker and simple unleavened bread for stick bread, damper goes in the ash or into the Dutch oven in the embers of the fire.

It is true everyone does collect in the kitchen at parties! The social experience of making food brings together groups. The same is true for children. Food allows them to build real relationships, to chat over their own method of making bread or how many berries the group picked. Let me at this point describe our Kinder Kitchen, I've touched upon it a couple of times already. The Kinder Kitchen is an open fronted log construction designed to replicate the experience of being around the kitchen table of a busy family home.

It has an outdoor kitchen area with a surface at different levels to cater for the heights of children. The child side is raised so that the adult and child are at the same eye level. The large table is designed to be a family size, so the group can stand around it to make their bread. A cosy nest by the log stove completes the space. We have called our outdoor kitchen the Kinder Kitchen and it has made the experience I describe in this chapter complete since the harmony with Nature has gone through the full cycle. My vision is that this space comes to represent harmonisation with natures cycles, even down to the wood it is made from and the energy it uses.

The eating celebration takes time, it has an important status as a social learning space. Cloths are made by children, clay plates are made, fired, glazed and fired again to make them strong. The enamel mugs and real knives and forks are used to set the table. A gift from nature sits on the table to provoke conversation. On most days the candles are lit and children and adults share lunch together. More and more children choose to stay, the atmosphere is not hurried and is treated as core teaching time.

Children's direct involvement in the preparation of food is important. Stick bread made in the forest is individual so each child can eat their own. The Kinderkitchen has individual stainless steel bowls, child sized kitchen utensils and a recipe board designed to encourage child created recipes. Within this environment are the numerous levels of order that prevail in everyday life.

The use of technology is in context. Grain grinders allow the children to grind their own corn or oats to add to the flour mixtures, bread and jam makers are programmed, cooking happens in a real oven. Digital thermometers are used to test food temperature, microwave digital technology is understood through use.

The landscape of the outdoor garden space has a purpose in terms of the planting, it is a polytunnel created by bending green stems. There is a cover to keep the deer and rabbits at bay. The rebuilding of the tunnel every couple of years has a positive effect in terms of re-establishing ownership of the area for re-current groups. Each design varies, each year new decisions are made about vegetables within a backdrop of perennial shrubs like redcurrants, black currants, hops and blackberries. When we first explored the children's relationship to fruit on trees, it became very evident that children had limited awareness of where the fruit came from, this is no longer the case.

The sustainable approach runs through everything we do. Mary Pipher in her book, 'The Shelter of Each Other', describes a lifestyle that is very familiar to an increasing number of young children all over the world. 'Many children today find it easier to stay indoors and watch television. I worry that children do not know what they are missing. Children cannot love what they do not know. They cannot miss what they have not experienced'. Our role is to create a sustainable method of connecting children with nature through many routes, from awe and wonder, to construction for shelters to food.

The moments that children have in early connections to nature may well remain as an emotion that carries children through to a place where they then go on to explore sustainability in later life. When we work with children we are using experience to build up threads of consciousness. For example, there is a given that the food waste will be composted. The compost cone gives an underground option which takes away the risk of vermin and since it requires no emptying it is easy for staff of a busy centre to manage.

The uncooked unsalted vegetable waste goes into the wormery or into the composting barrel. The collection of the 'magic energy food' from the base of the wormery and its application to the vegetable and fruit areas is very important so that children see the cycle of material in a practical way. Flower pots are made from newspaper not from plastic. The process of scrubbing the earthenware pots is linked to the closing down of the garden area ready for winter. The organic management of the food area allows children to be fully involved, companion planting, drip feed systems, some hydroponics are used within the space when appropriate. The details of setup are in the book entitled Journeys into Nature.

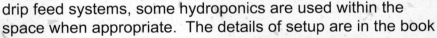

The way that the garden space gives us produce is only one of its features, the awe and wonder of an apple growing is also celebrated. The blackcurrant bush leaves make their way into petal perfume because of their pungent smell. The wooden clippings are used for art work. The re-use

of as many facets of the space give a real sense of what sustainability means making what you do effective so it can go on. Putting back minerals should not happen with chemicals but core planting programmes, so that children realise that nature has the balance. If we work in harmony we can make our lives easier and of course healthier.

Wool based compost can be used that is processed locally. The use of peat would certainly be avoided, due to the reduction of peat bog habitats around the world. Children can easily understand links and impacts of actions in this way.

Children can handle all natural materials and therefore become fully involved in the preparation, planting, tending, harvesting and processing. Discussions occur about pests and disease, the cycles of life and the importance of food.

Case Study: 'Potatoes'

Children in the centre were exploring roots, root vegetables and in particluar were interested in potatoes. A large bag of assorted potatoes was brought into the centre. Children sorted these using complex sorting criteria including a collection of only perfectly oval shapes, colour, smell, texture and by the shape and number of sprouting roots! Comments about the roots were; "wibbly worms on it", "Look this is a weird one, it is like a worm coming out of it".

A 4 year old girl only wanted the pink potatoes. She went on to slice a potato into many thin slices to count how many crisps she could make using her potato. Some children lined the potatoes up

by size, others looked for the potatoes with the most interesting shapes; "Snowman and a pig shape - that one is my favourite". Children used torches to look closely at the potatoes. One 4 year old boy commented; "I am the potato sorter, my name is potato sorter".

The adult asked what would happen if the potatoes were put in the garden? "Roots need to be sticking up", "We need a seed", "If we plant all of them we will have so many", "Sometimes they don't, sometimes", "This one is yucky". A 4 year old girl used her knife to open the potato to see why it was 'yucky'. "I can't see a worm", "Is it a spider?", "Cut it again, cut it in half again", "That's a quarter then". The learning naturally evolved linked in its concepts and knowledge, along a flexible pathway to allow interest points to be followed.

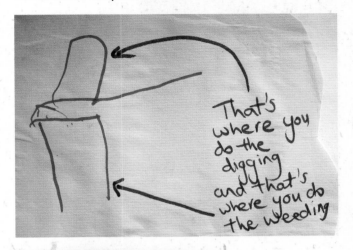

That's where you do the digging and that's where you do the weeding

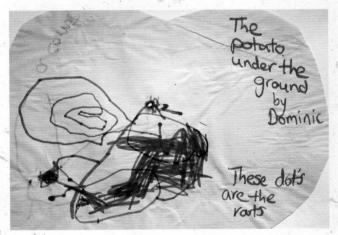

The potato under the ground by Dominic

These dots are the roots

Children planted the potatoes in the garden. A 4 year old boy planted his by order of size as he wanted the plants to grow by height order.

A daily chart was made recording the growth of the potato plants and children commented on the small white flowers. A few plants were dug out too early with children then making the decision that they needed to grow bigger.

A decision was made by the children that the plants were now big enough and the whole group took part in the harvesting of potatoes. "You have to dig and dig and then you find one", "They grow under the ground all stuck together", "we can cook them, we can take them home and mummy can cook them", " I found one, it is dirty, I have to wash it now".

All the children from the 2 year olds to the 5 year olds enjoyed washing and again sorting the new potatoes. One 4 year old made the observation that none of their potatoes "had those wiggly bits sticking out". Children took some of the potatoes home to share with their families.

At Auchlone Nature Kindergarten the children were keen to make a stew using the little potatoes. They helped to cut them up into small pieces, peeled and then chopped and added carrots and tomatoes. Children decided on the amount of water that was needed to make the best sauce and this was added. The Dutch Oven was placed on the fire and children went off to play.

They started to move back once they could smell the stew. "It smells good, like potatoes", "We are cooking like mummy and daddy, making dinner".

The enjoyment of the children when they sat around the fire to eat their own stew was obvious and children who would not normally eat some of the ingredients were keen to eat what they had created themselves. Practical experiences of nature as the provider are powerful, but it is also important that children understand the cycle to put back what we have not used, or leave what we do not need.

Key Points:

Children create a deep rooted connection to the earth when they are able to connect to it in a variety of ways.

Nature can provide a store cupboard of materials that can be used in a learning space if the centre works in harmony with nature for long term sustainability.

Nature Kindergartens work in harmony with nature from the food they eat in season, to materials grown for creative use, to changing experiences in the wild woods with the seasons.

Chapter 10

A place where people work in 'Nature Time'

'Adopt the pace of nature; her secret is patience'.

Ralph Waldo Emerson

Every curriculum document that I read has mention of some form of outdoor learning, in some it sits in the methodology section, in others it can be found in the physical outcomes. There are however, very few who touch on it to influence the pace of learning and the way that we should be protecting time for children to learn in 'nature time'. Time for children to learn at their pace, to explore and experiment is vital if their sensory systems are to help them learn.

This experience of pressure seems to be especially true in Western cultures, where for the sake of objective understandings, children are encouraged to focus their learning on cognitive models rather than on first-hand investigations of the natural environment. Cognitive models encourage children to make a transition from reliance on sensory criteria as a way of knowing the world to cognitive criteria, and in the process, construct a more objective or scientific understanding of the natural environment.

Such a transition carries with it a heavy price, including both a physical and psychological separation from the environment. 'As a result, the child goes from an adaptive and sympathetic attitude to a critical and analytical one... The child no longer creates a concept of the world from experience but rather receives it from others. The child's individual, multidimensional world becomes a scientific one, identical to that of his/her friends' (Sebba, 1991).

The physical and psychological separation from the environment that accompanies the transition from the child's ways of knowing the world deserves careful reflection and discussion by early childhood educators and child development specialists. The lens of cognition through which most adults view the world has serious limitations. Through this lens, we see no more than 'a defective second edition' (Bialik, 1938), far removed from the child's way of seeing the world. As we move from childhood into adulthood, our receptivity diminishes. A child's way of knowing allows him or her to 'linger in self-forgetfulness... she is all eyes and ears. Nor is she projecting anything, nor generalizing or classifying' (Hinchman, 1991), as adults are inclined to do.

The richness of young children's way of perceiving the world is based, in part, on their gift of primal seeing. Rather than being incorrect or inferior, primal seeing allows children to experience the 'embodiment of things, their very quintessence' (Bialik, 1938/1939). For most people, primal seeing is experienced only during childhood, so it would be good and right and beautiful for parents and early childhood educators to honour and celebrate this way of knowing and experiencing the natural world rather than pushing children to let go of it.

Failing to recognise and support children's ways of knowing can have serious implications on how they will relate to the natural world over the span of their lifetime. Shaw-Jones (1992), would ask us to consider 'the way we think, the mental maps that we construct to make meaning of the world, affect the way we feel about it, and the way we behave toward it'. By validating and reinforcing the child's ways of knowing, we will be fostering a life-long love of the natural world. By failing to do so, we could be contributing to the increasingly more complex environmental crisis, which is considered to be due, in a large part to a growing psychological detachment from and prejudice against nature (Cohen, 1984; Devall, 1984/85; Raglon, 1993). By forcing the child to work prematurely with abstract thought, we 'break up the vital unity of self and world'. (Pearce, 1977).

The pace of projected learning has been steadily getting faster. Children are being moved through childhood at an alarming rate. The concept of 'lingering days' with elements of boredom within them, that in turn would provocate creativity, appear to have disappeared. Children in the UK can enter an education system from 4 yrs old, although the entry programmes in Scotland and Wales allow this to be before 6 years old.

Early years environments in schools are trying to create harmonious, home like spaces, but they are still institutions that run the risk of 'creating norms' in society. As Cobb (1977), suggests there is a real link between both creativity and a positive attitude to the earth in adults who have an inner memory map rooted in nature. Four years old is a very pliable age full of experiences, the effect of nature and its freedom is very influential at this point.

Children need the opportunity to revisit over time, not just a few moments after but at time frames that mean something to them. The meta-cognition that is developed through looking back to reflect is a powerful tool. The day that the little boy said that he had now learned that aliens don't have rhubarb heads is significant and should be able to be seen in documentation for adults and made visible to the child and his peers. The key learning moments actually took place eight months after the rhubarb had first been noticed. Nature will work at its pace and it is we who have to adjust to it. The Floorbooks carry thoughts across seasons, across years in some cases, but also within an hour. The flexibility of the system has to reflect the unpredictability of the natural world.

I was asked about the pressure of time recently and although as adults many of us cannot think of a time without a deadline or a structure, it is so important that we protect the time of childhood. Children are part of nature and as such they should work in that time frame not one of over organised targets and schedules of entertainment.

Case Study: 'Alien Rhubarb'

"There's an alien in the garden," a 3 year old boy shouted as he arrived at the kindergarten one morning. On closer examination he had discovered the pink and wrinkled growth of a rhubarb plant emerging through the fresh soil. "It's all coming up, crinkles everywhere, scrunchy, brown, yucky", were some of the comments made by children.

Over the next few weeks this plant became a focus point in the centre with children observing the unfurling of the leaves and slow straightening of the stem until they themselves identified it as a rhubarb plant. The children observed that slugs loved to hide under the leaves and regularly lifted the leaves up, so that the ducks could find the hidden slugs.

Children watched the flowers growing out of the centre of the plant and measured the height against themselves. When they harvested the rhubarb, they used the giant leaves as hiding places. "Mine is the biggest", "Mine is bigger than my head", "I hide with you". Children discovered that leaves left overnight or in the sun became limp and soft which led to an exploration of fluid loss and evaporation. "Mine can't stand up, I want it to go up".

One 4 year old boy looked at the size of the leaf and the length of the stem; "Is it ready to eat?" Children learnt that rhubarb leaves are poisonous but the stems can be eaten.

A 3 year old boy commented, "My mummy cuts it and we cook it and that makes rhubarb crumble. We need sugar and raisins". A 4 year old boy replied; "No, we don't need raisins - you don't put raisins in a pudding. We need flour and sugar and I like cinnamon. That is like brown powder but it tastes nice". Other children commented; "I have cinnamon on my pancakes, cinnamon and sugar", "I like pancakes", I have pancakes - my mummy makes pancakes... yummy". Children created recipes and wrote lists of ingredients and quantities - we did manage to cook and eat some of the recipes produced ....other recipes were destined to fail!

Leaves left on the plant turned yellow and holes appeared, children counted the holes and looked for the culprits causing them. A 4 year old girl commented; " This leaf is full of holes. I think a slug must have eaten it". A 4 year old boy replied; "or a snail, snails eat leaves too". A 3 year old girl observed; "One red one, one brown one, lots of yellow ones". The 4 year old boy added; "they go brown when they are dead"

"It's soft - ugg, I don't like it, slugs won't eat it now!" "I think the slugs have eaten this one - they made a peep hole!" "I can see you in there".

Eventually the brown, slimy and decomposed leaves were removed by the children and added to the compost bin. They periodically looked to see if a new rhubarb plant would appear.

A year after the first discovery the same boy who was now 4 years old came striding in one morning, "It's back and I know it looks like an alien but it isn't ...it's rhubarb!"

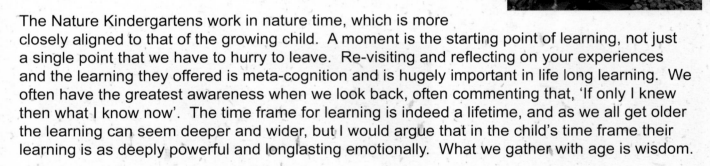

The complete investigation took a whole year from the emergence of the first leaves, to the decomposition and then the emergence of the new leaves.

The Nature Kindergartens work in nature time, which is more closely aligned to that of the growing child. A moment is the starting point of learning, not just a single point that we have to hurry to leave. Re-visiting and reflecting on your experiences and the learning they offered is meta-cognition and is hugely important in life long learning. We often have the greatest awareness when we look back, often commenting that, 'If only I knew then what I know now'. The time frame for learning is indeed a lifetime, and as we all get older the learning can seem deeper and wider, but I would argue that in the child's time frame their learning is as deeply powerful and longlasting emotionally. What we gather with age is wisdom.

Key Points:

Children need time to think, to explore and assimilate.

There should be a celebration of the uniqueness of childhood and the thinking processes it holds.

Responding to children's style and pace of learning will enable their links to nature to be deep rooted.

Metacognitive strategies should be applied to any learning journey for children.

Chapter 11
A place of journeys and transitions

'...In every walk with nature one receives far more than he seeks'.

John Muir

The most wonderful provision for all children would be to place early years centres in natural spaces, where the air quality is high and the children have a sense of freedom from beginning to end. The reality is that in many parts of the world we are all trying to create harmonious care for children in a wide variety of spaces. Some Forest School projects involve children going by bus to a local woodland site, others walk to a site most have some kind of journey. The journey to get to nature will be part of that learning experience. Let us think about, however, the environmental impact of children going into natural spaces every day on the same pathway and the effect this will have on the land. The compaction of the ground they walk on, suppresses new growth, the repeated use of an area may prevent the natural succession of plants into the space; the denudation of trees, grass and flowers can be rapid when large numbers of children use an area all day every day. The aspect of journeying offers us a number of possibilities to minimise the impact on the very space we are trying to connect to.

On our sites, the journey into the woods or wild space is part of the preparation that the children really enjoy. Each child has a rucksack and they are responsible for putting in hat, gloves, food and drink. To support the independence of the children, there should be systems that empower them. Research in this area would demonstrate this empowerment. The creation of a rucksack peg stand or a peg tree, enables children to store their sacks and revisit them when they need their belongings.

When you start to see children playing in more natural open spaces where there is a feeling of wildness, one starts to see that animals and children actually follow similar desires. The hidden path, the path that leads to food, the path that leads to excitement, the path that leads to a meeting place, the path that leads to a hiding place and the path that leads to home. The feeling of being on an adventure is thrilling, it has with it a real feeling of anticipation going off into a different space. The adventure in adult terms may be up a short path, but to those children it is a mountainous trek. Climbing a short embankment is the ascent of Everest and so therefore, the feeling of achievement can be as great and affective in terms of the development of self esteem.

Similar behaviours have been seen at the Nature Kindergartens. Signage, ways of marking their place were predominant from wooden signs naming spaces, such as the Wild Wood, or the Low Den, the Fungi Garden or the Splitting Space (where two paths divide). The signs are always made from materials that will biodegrade, so that over time the names can change with new groups of children. Traditional names are part of the history of a play space, but permanency of ownership and naming of all areas of the space can really limit the aspiration of those children that come after.

Pathways have become significant. The design process and their decisions require a great deal of thought and are so very complex.

• The movement direction and style children discuss should they go around objects or over, to crawl along or to leap and run. The features of the pathway such as rumble strips of branches to walk over, burglar traps, arches both for welcome and defence.

• The length of the journey and duration through time. The children want to go on for so long to make you 'just so tired' or to be short 'because we need time to cook marshmallows' or 'just a wee one because some people have little legs'.

• The degree of risk fluctuates. The rope climb to the top of the knoll or the gentle stroll around in a spiral to the top is dictated by the energy levels on the day and throughout the day. Morning session can see great adrenaline, whilst the afternoon becomes more about 'strolling and wandering'.

• The direction generally within the site, to a destination such as to the 'Dark Den', the 'Climbing Tree', 'the Dragon' is decided by the children unless the weather dictates they go in another direction. In which case there has to be a meeting at the 'Singing Tree'. The routine of revisiting a space gives the children a real connection that allows them to see and experience the changes in nature. The flexibility of different pathways, as I mentioned above, allows the ground to rest.

Meeting trees and way markers are an effective way to give children some freedom, whilst putting in some boundaries for supervision. The trees have characters that children have noticed in their play, such as the 'Singing Tree', the 'Fairy Tree', the 'Bouncing Tree'. At the Waldkindergarten it was interesting to note a similarity in play that the children in the public woods also had names for meeting places and some had been named years ago by their parents, for example, the 'Lion Tree' that has a mark about ten feet up.

The pathways into the wild woods from both spaces have been changed over time. The entrance way into the space is a rite of passage, a transition is often marked with an archway, a sculpture and so forth. A group of children at Auchlone had decided to make a new pathway, 'a second roadway to

go up the hill'. The creation of the archway started the process, with a series of arrows fashioned out of sticks to mark the way. The clearing of the path lead to a request to define the edge, which was not something the adults would have considered. The children moved long branches along the edge to 'keep people in and to stop us falling off' and 'to show people where to go'. Perhaps it is an experience of paths, perhaps a need for enclosure. It is still an interesting focus for the team to explore to understand the child need for a system in a space that we felt could be free of them!

The autonomy of choosing your own route is of interest to us as a group. When the children designed the way into the centre they talked about having a separate way in to the garden, away from their parents. So their designs for a gate, bridge and tunnel were created. Many younger children enjoy the passage through a boundary which is one of a number of schemas or repeatable patterns of behaviour as outlined by Cathy Nutbrown (2006). The entrance way into the Nature Kindergarten is a focal point for the youngest children and they do spend some time going over the bridge, back through the gate, and through the tunnel with such a look of satisfaction on their faces. The staff at Earlham Early Years Centre in England, talk of a 'gate to somewhere', I would agree, and yet sometimes I

wonder if it is a gate to nowhere and then back again! The observation of younger children under three, helps us to understand their access and connection to the sense of wildness. It is certainly a place of high opportunity for play with loose materials. The younger children of two years old often take a comforter with them in their back packs, they collect and gather objects throughout the journey and relocate them further on at settling points that they, as a group, have defined as a good place to be. We have noticed their ability to find a low log of a perfect size for

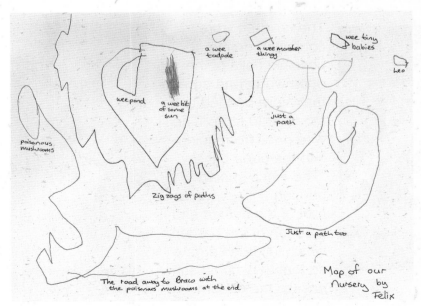

Map of our Nursery by Felix

their legs. Their favourite is the one at the edge of the hill that gradually slopes to give grades of height, so each child can find their perfect seat. They can rest on their journey either at the hammock site, or in a hammock that the adults take with them on the journey.

The connection between the group is significant on their journeys, the patience to stop and wait, the unhurried pace so that they stay together as a group, the helping hand, or advice given, all create a supportive space for gentle peer mentoring.

Case study: 'Building a Barrier'

The large body of water near the forest site has bush cover around it which creates a barrier in the summer. In the winter there is a more open line of access. It was agreed to work with the children to erect a fence from the wood supply around us. The fence line was decided by the topography of the land, moving around the trees, bushes and logs. The safety parameters of

deep water require clear procedures, one option would be higher staff child ratio, the other is to define and protect the edge so that access is controlled. It was decided to go with the latter and then create an area where children go through with the adult awareness.

The children were consulted on the possible risks of the open water and agreed that there needed to be a barrier to stop; "The wee ones from going into the deep bits", "The fence should be high". They were part of the design and creation of the barrier which included a gate so that they could still access the stream.

'The fence should be high'

by Rosalind

The adults put in the outline posts for strength and then the children wove sticks and branches in and out of the posts after collecting, sorting and lining up the sticks.

Two boys fetched a tape measure, "We need to measure", "A measuring tape to measure trees and things". They measured one metre lengths, marked the sticks and sawed them to size. Children of all ages worked together.

There is a small rill, that runs along the side of the site and it offers an opportunity for water play. The area next to the water was cleared a little so that both banks were visible. The grass area was enlarged with the line of the fence coming out from the slope to allow space for group access and play, and children included small gates in their designs.

One 4 year old boy felt that the frame needed to be tied together with string, "I've done it. I tied a knot! It stops it from blowing away", "I just tangled it up and then tied it, then I tied it under and out again and did the same things again", "Get a piece of string and tie it in a knot like this, cross your arms and put the one that was under over them, and that's how you tie a knot!"

A 2 year old boy and 3 year old girl, decorated the fence using leaves, first placing them onto the fence and then pushing the leaves down onto the sticks creating a hole so that the leaf would not fly away. Other children joined them and the fence was decorated with an assortment of threaded leaves attached to the twigs and brances.

One 4 year old boy surveyed the completed fence, "I like this fence a lot because it has a lot of branches. You know all of these branches, each of these branches, well, there's probably 100 branches in this fence, maybe more! I am going to count how many branches in each square. Seven!"

By empowering and consulting with children throughout the whole process they were able to transfer their gained knowledge to other areas of the Kindergarten and went on to create more

barriers to protect natural places special to them from damage, either from children or wildlife, by creating similar barriers judging the required height and construction necessary to adequately protect the environments. The wildlife pond within the garden space, the aconites and any new saplings are surrounded by mini barriers designed and created by the children. They also create similar barriers in their play to build fences for farms or miniature fences for the fairies.

The dynamic of a group of children gathering together to prepare themselves mentally and physically, to organise themselves and then experience the departure, moments of settling or happenings and the return to base are indeed all part of the journey. In fact, perhaps we should also include the memories we gather and process afterwards that serve to keep the journey alive.

Key Points:

The journey is often as important as the destination.

Adventurous journeys' give children experience of change to seek out new things. They draw on this emotion when they are ready to take a step on their own.

Humans seem to need to feel that they have a had a 'presence' in a place and time.

The awareness of boundaries is a human desire. Children in Nature Kindergartens have far reaching boundaries that allow them to explore their own capabilities.

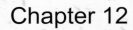

Chapter 12
A place with access to the 'wild'

'The miracle is not to fly in the air, or to walk on the water, but to 'really' walk on the earth'.

Chinese Proverb

What is a wild space? Is it a place where we feel wild and free or a place that nature is free? Travelling gives one a real sense of how people engage with nature. We can see nature hanging on, trying to grow in the most amazing spaces. Buddlea bushes high up on the church steeple, grass in gutters even bird nests on telegraph posts. Is nature trying to tell us something, we destroy it and it heals itself, bringing itself back when it has time to respond and adapt?

In the western culture there has been such a move towards containing and controlling nature that you can go up mountains completely removed from the very elements you are going up there to feel. Do people travel in a car or train through a natural space to connect to nature or merely to conquer it and then say it has been claimed?

Humans can be so removed from the 'realness of nature'. Nature is presented to them. Ant farms in a box, rather than in their garden. Mud face packs in a packet rather than feeling it outside. Produce from nature processed in such a way that it does not resemble its original form.

It is almost as if we are trying to offer 'canned nature'. Nature presented on our terms, to meet our comfort zone. Materials are collected and gathered, and then beautifully presented inside. It will indeed be beautiful, stunning in the complexity of materials but it is still removed from its natural space which is 'in natural surroundings'. Details can become more focussed when we change the way we look at the materials, when we look in detail at the micro elements of a substance, we can open our eyes to an amazing secret world. Yet surely there needs to be a balance. A place where children meet nature in its own space, spaces where there are connections between the shell and the sand, the rose and the thorn, the leaf and its tree. Contextual relationships are important since they support the way that things connect and interrelate. They allow children to make their own natural connections and put together frameworks of understanding about the world around them.

Some methodologies suggest that we should over simplify or create abstract experiences to ensure the child can 'do' something. Is this the way our brains really take on board information? Should education be about simplifying 'main ideas' to make them almost a myth or, should we encourage children to think deeply from an early age? I have seen people spray cobwebs with hairspray or sprinkled talc on to put them onto paper, to bring inside. So what does this say to children? That we have the right to remove an essential part of a spiders existence, or that it's okay since the spider will just make another one? A task that is as big as us building a tree house. Wild spaces are just that, a place to be connected to nature in a natural way, a wild way. It is not an adult designed landscape area although through time, a well thought out space can become wild.

Wild natural spaces, are disorderly, free ranging, and untidy...this surely adds to the attraction to children as spaces that are within their domain (Heerwagen and Orians 2002). Children show by their enthusiasm for the wild spaces that they offer a different experience. If we take the three spaces of naturalistic inside, landscaped space as the garden and then the wild area there should be a development of challenge. Skills learned inside or in the garden can be applied in more open ended ways in the wild space. Let us just qualify what we mean here by a wild space in terms of behaviour. It is a space that does have boundaries. The boundaries are negotiated, and therefore understood by the children in the space. The open, consultative adults that work in this space are about connection, relationship and harmony within the group. This does not mean that there is never disequilibrium, there

is in that moment clear evidence of deep level learning that a facilitator can bring forward in discussions.

The space that children play in has an influence on them and they have an effect on it, both real and perceived. When there is this element then true play, full of autonomy, can take place. When strong adult rules start to overtake play, then some of the integrity and the true nature of play will be compromised, children start to work in a culture of rules rather than empowerment. The balance for many educational principles is that the curriculum is not defined by children. It is created by people with another agenda. Practitioners all over the world, do however, have the choice as to the methodology of delivery of many programmes. Some of those people choose to deliver a curriculum of experience in 'wild spaces'.

Early experiences with the natural world have also been positively linked with the sense of wonder. 'Wonder', as described by Cobb (1977), is not an abstract term or a lofty ideal. It is instead, a phenomenon concretely rooted in the child's developing perceptual capabilities and his or her ways of knowing. This way of knowing, if recognised and honoured, can serve as a life-long source of joy and enrichment, as well as an impetus, or motivation, for further learning (Carson 1956). If we explore the difference between a found experience and one that has been planned and presented, there is a difference in the child's response. To come upon an otter in a stream is so far removed from staring at one in a

zoo. The experience of closely studying an insect can be exciting, but it would have more relevance to understanding nature if the experience was looking at local flora and fauna that are as amazing as some of those taken around schools in cages.

Are wild spaces for Nature Kindergartens only in the woods? Well, in the Scandinavian and northern European countries that could be seen to be true, due to the landscape they have around them. There are however, links to the water, to beaches, to marsh areas to a wide variety of environments. The development of a nature kindergarten in a dry sandy part of the world is my current project. To support the staff there to see beyond their feeling that 'they have no nature' is a critical part of the work I now do. The image of nature is

often one of Flora, and yet the wind is part of nature. Let us not forget that the intense cold of the arctic tundra has families who live upon it and so they have created a way of working in harmony with nature in these more remote wild spaces.

The greatest challenge is to look at the urbanised areas where there can be a great deal of safety surface, vandalism and loss of connection to the beauty of nature. For these children large scale experiences may well take place through a journey to a naturalistic play park on the outside of the city, just as the original Danish centres.

.
As this book is being written, the Scottish government is defining the parameters of funding to bring back naturalistic play into the lives of the children in Scotland. The journey has taken a long time, from lobbying, writing, and training to raise the awareness of the need to be outside, that started twenty years ago to this point, where naturalistic spaces are now being promoted, has involved many frustrating discussions and challenges. So perhaps there is a really positive moment here where we can say that we are protecting childhood.

Case Study: 'Dancing in the Wind'

Wild spaces offer children the opportunity to move freely and closely experience nature in its raw state whether this is on grassland, woodland or the beach. Two 4 year old girls were digging on the beach using their hands and commenting on the warm surface sand

changing to cooler damp sand as they dug deeper. They moulded the damp sand with their hands and feet and rubbed the sand against their skin commenting on the roughness. One little girl sat back and turned her face towards the sun and wind. Closing her eyes she enjoyed the sensation of the sun's heat as well as the wind touching her face and

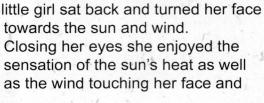

moving through her hair. She slowly stood up and started to dance and move with the wind, flinging her arms out wide and twirling and turning. Her friend watched for a minute and then joined in the spontaneous dance. Their dance moved them into the shallow water where they picked up two sea shells which they included in their dance, throwing them ahead and dancing after them. They created a game all of their own dancing in the waves, moving with the wind and watching their shadows and reflection in the water moving with them. They were using all their senses to delight in nature.

Key Points:

Humans need to allow themselves the time to feel a sense of wildness to put other aspects of living into perspective.

'Canned nature' is not the same experience as being connected to nature overtime.

Wild spaces are disorderly, free ranging and therefore, a challenge to fit into traditional quality assurance models.

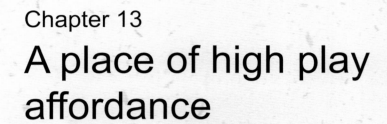

Chapter 13
A place of high play affordance

'*We depend on the gifts of nature, but these gifts must be received with gratitude but not exploited or abused*'.

Satish Kumar

If we have ever met, we will have probably shared a moment looking at some images of ducks! The clip art imagery of received learning as compared to an old stick from the Island of Bute in Scotland, that has multifaceted layers of learning within it. This chapter will take forward some of the points from research that sit behind the work that we promote. The research is empirical and wide ranging which gives a solid foundation to talk of play and learning in naturalistic spaces

One of the strengths of nature is in its open ended resources and limitless experiences that it offers to children. Closed, overdesigned, usually plastic resources offer very few play affordances for children. Why is this so? And further what implications does this have for our practice?

When given the opportunity, children physically demonstrate preference, and enjoy playing in natural environments and/or with natural elements (Hart 1979; Moore 1986; Chawla 2002; Heerwagen and Orians 2002; Burke 2005). The wealth of research shows that they do so because of the over-whelming play potential of such spaces; the possibilities of now and the promise of more to come (Cobb 1977). Imagine the emotion of a child that has no promise or enticement of 'more to come'. Perhaps disconnection, boredom, lack of drive, in fact multiple behaviours that we are observing in early years environments that are 'over resourced', with too much visual clutter, or in soft play areas with no colour harmony, or in programmes that are over structured to give no room for a child's 'voice' to grow.

The concept of 'affordances' (Gibson 1979), refers to what the environment offers, what it provides for the child. Affordances are opportunities that arise from the interaction between the physical properties of the environment and the interests, ideas and intent of the individual. If the physical environment is overdesigned and organised it limits the very play it is trying to encourage. Affordances arise through active detection, where the person is both sensing and moving, observing and acting at the same time. Kytta has done some great work on this (2002, 2004, 2006).

Applying the concept of affordance to children's play in natural environments has a number of points to reflect upon:

• Affordances are unique to the individual playing child or group of children and are to some extent unpredictable. Children play in an environment and have an effect on it, whilst at the same point, the environment is affecting the child.

• Affordances are highly dynamic – different features, elements, materials affording different play experiences for different individuals on different occasions. Every day is different, the moisture, temperature, light, movement in natural spaces is changing constantly, stimulating new ideas and persectives.

• The number of affordances increases with complexity of the environment. As highly complex environments, natural spaces provide limitless play affordances. Children who play in nature are imaginative because the stimulation is constantly stimulating the brain.

• Combinations of affordances allow individual or group play lines to develop naturally. Children can attach a joint meaning to a moment or indeed an object, they can hold it which is a fishing rod to one and a giraffe neck to another.

• Natural environments afford children with coherent opportunities to play with feelings and emotions through playing in wild natural spaces, children can encounter and experience fear, disgust, disappointment and anger as well as delight, fascination, satisfaction and contentment within a protected world of play based activity. (Lester and Russell,2007).

Nabhan and Trimble (1994), in The Geography of Childhood, present a compelling discussion as to why children need access to natural places and what we might do to assure children frequent opportunities for interacting with the world of nature. They suggest that a logical place to start is rethinking the concept of playgrounds. As Nabhan (1994) says: 'To counter the historic trend toward the loss of wildness where children play, it is clear that we need to find ways to let children roam beyond the pavement, to gain access to vegetation and earth that allows them to tunnel, climb, or even fall. And because formal playgrounds are the only outdoors that many children experience anymore, should we be paying more attention to planting, and less to building on them?'.

Natural places match children's ways of knowing in that they offer varied opportunities for adventure, construction, and re-invention. The 'rough ground' aspects of natural places offer the 'qualities of openness, diversity, manipulation, explorability, anonymity, and wildness... the indeterminacy of rough ground allows it to become a play-partner, like other forms of creative partnership, actress-audience, potter-clay, photographer-subject, painter-canvas. The exploring/creating child is not making 'art' so much as using the landscape as a medium for understanding the world' (Moore, quoted in Trimble, 1994).

Junk yard playgrounds in Israel, Denmark and Melbourne in Australia, have been designed to create a high play affordance through man-made materials. The scrap store or Re-Mida centres in Italy are linked to this concept. Some outdoor consultants have created landscapes of found materials. It does seem ironic to me that some are now manufacturing a new version of an old bread crate that was collected to reduce land fill! Open ended play materials do not 'need' to be natural, but if they are they will be richer and have less environmental impact.

The nature of our work is to look to design wild spaces with naturally occurring materials for additional ethical reasons surrounding sustainability, visual harmony and the sheer beauty within natures fascinating variation.

So what would the features of this wild space be? Nature of course, but there are easy elements to consider for both their beauty, purpose and of course play value. Ward (1988), uses the example of trees to offer a large number of potential play affordances. Trees can be climbed and hidden behind, they can become forts or bases, with their surrounding vegetation and roots, they become dens and little houses, they provide shelter, landmarks and privacy, fallen, they become part of an obstacle course or material for denbuilding; near them you find birds, little animals, conkers, fallen leaves, mud, fir cones and winged seeds; they provide a suitable backdrop for every conceivable game of the imagination. (Ward1988).

Furthermore, natural environments containing many different species will extend the affordances of that space. For example, different trees drop their leaves at different times, produce different types of fruits and seeds, and their roots, trunks and branches grow in different ways. The bark and the very essence of trees is so very different. I am reminded of a little boy who told me that every tree has a different song. What he had discovered was that his stick created a new sound according to the tree species, its size and age (growth rate). At 2 years old, he had limited formal language that would explain the different growth rates of species and the effect of climate, or that the xylem and phloem inside the tree were acting as resonance tubes, but he did intuitively understand and demonstrate in his play that they were all different because of what lay inside.

To design naturalistic playscapes requires a real understanding of what it is that motivates children. Stuart Lester's work (2006), suggests that children are naturally good at finding affordances, they are 'affordance connoisseurs', and through playing outdoors, seek to maximise affordances such as creating playful problems for themselves.

In our Nature Kindergartens, whether on a beach, in a meadow or in a forest, all make use of the idea of natural materials to allow the maximum amount of play affordances. The case study that accompanies this chapter is a wonderful example of practitioners, both understanding play affordances whilst considering the delicate nature of play and their role within it.

Case Study: 'Transformational Play'

During a study visit to a Wald Kindergarten in Germany we were able to experience the same transformational play we observe when our children spend long uninterrupted periods of time in the woodlands of our Scottish Kindergartens.

A group of children were adding an extension to a boat they had been working on during previous visits to the woodland space. During the selecting and adding specially chosen bits of wood, the boat became a spaceship. One 5 year old boy found a shaped piece of wood that was then used as a drill, the nozzle for the petrol pump and a laser gun.

He wandered away looking for a seat for the spaceship and came back with a large piece of wood and proudly announced, "This is for me to hang my clothes on, my hat goes there and my coat on this hook".

A friend commented that it looked like a giraffe, he created a tail for it using pine needles, pretended to feed it leaves and then ride on it. A 3 year old girl was invited to have a ride and she announced that 'It was a very good horse!'

When it was time to go back to the centre, the boy wanted to take his giraffe with him. The ethos of the

Kindergarten allowed children this choice and it was his responsibility to get it back to the centre. He started off pulling it along behind him and when he got tired, a friend offered to help him carry it. The staff supported them verbally as appropriate, did not rush them but also did not make any suggestions to ease the task such as using a rope to pull it along. They felt that the children knew where the ropes were and would come to that conclusion themselves when they were ready!

After 10 minutes the boy stopped, told the adult that he needed a rope, tied the rope to the giraffe and dragged it behind him. As the energy now required to pull it was so much less, he was soon able to run ahead of the group. A little girl stopped him, sat on the piece of wood and it was transformed into a sledge which was easily pulled along the icy ground.

On arrival at the centre, the little boy removed the rope, placed the piece of wood next to the door and proudly announced, "This is my coat rack and this is where I put my hat and this is the hook for my coat". Play provides the opportunity for flexibility and variation that is full of boundless possibilities. These examples of transformational play give us a window into the journeys of thinking that children are on through time and space.

Key Points:

Landscapes with high play affordance offer the greatest learning potential.

Nature based landscapes are more environmentally friendly and sustainable than those that are over clutterred by plastic closed materials.

The majority of children have a natural ability to understand the nature of open play and the play affordances it gives.

Chapter 14

A place to explore the interconnectedness of the earth

'The grand show is eternal. It is always sunrise somewhere; the dew is never dried all at once; a shower is forever falling; vapor is ever rising. Eternal sunrise, eternal dawn and gloaming, on sea and continents and islands, each in its turn, as the round earth rolls'.

John Muir

Children have a natural understanding of the world around them and therefore have a fascination with all aspects of it. Children from an early age are explorers and they have a natural enquiring mind that will lead them to ask the most fundamental and yet thought provoking questions. One of the perennial discussions is around how far the questions are allowed to go and how real the experience should be.

In many cultures around the world there are behavioural codes that weave respect for the land through all their work, for some the place of nature is central to their lives and also to their spirituality. The Maori culture has a link to the earth, and holds a huge body of knowledge about the plants, animals and the balance of the natural elements. The onset of commercialism has created a distance for many people from nature and the impact their actions have upon it. Children in many groups are removed from the experience of grief, in an adult attempt to protect them from it when they are 'so young'. In our experience nature provides natural moments to explore the cycle of life, a case study of this is detailed below.

Nature can be harsh and unyielding as well as calm and beautiful. The experience of exploring issues such as death, decay, miracles of birth and survival, are all important and are still discussed by adults as the imponderables of life.

The cycle of nature is an aspect that we often discuss as a group. We look at how children use the forest when they are there every day. There was a tendency to look at the creations they had made like a xylophone and consider fixing it, maintaining it for longevity and then we realised that we were fixing it for us, to see something in the forest. So now we leave it and if the string rots we talk about it, if fungus starts growing on it we talk about where it came from, if the system collapses, it is a wonderful opportunity to start again and redesign the space or find music in another way.

The other aspect we are trying to be mindful of is whether there are cues in the children's play that triggers the movement of group interest. The wild wood has many paths to many dens both current and abandoned. The dens are monitored for roof collapse but on the whole they are left for nature to reclaim. Magical moments do happen when small birds come in to shelter, or a deer scrapes a bed in the space enclosed by children. What makes the play move on? Is the area of space too large for a deeper level of engagement, or is the repetitive den play we observe in small outdoor areas simply a product of lack of space? At least two role play areas in centres do seem to have a deepening affect on the engagement and storying observed. If children had more indoor and garden space would this expand to five or six as it has in the wood?

The understanding of decay and change is very vividly seen in the way that mushrooms and fungi move in to start the 'return to earth'. The dens are reclaimed and often over the year the children can see the decay taking hold on anything that is natural and is left to the elements of rain, snow and wind. Children are fascinated by changes in nature and fungi come and go so rapidly it is almost like time lapse photography.

Case Study: 'Fungi Knowledge'

Children came upon a variety of fungi in the woodland and a discussion about the differences took place, "A mouse eated these! It's long and has a big head", "These are spotty mushrooms", "I have mushrooms in my garden, but you can't eat them", "Some are flower shape and some snail shape". A 4 year old observed, "These two kinds of mushrooms are the same I think but different colours". He went off to fetch the fungi identification chart and identified them as Yellow Staghorns. A mushroom with holes was found, "Oh a bird or pheasant must of eated it".

One 3 year old girl with very little speech at the time, used a magnifying glass to look closely at some black fungi she had found. She compared them using the fungi ID chart and identified her fungi as 'Earth tongues', by pointing to the images on the chart and nodding her head.

The children went back to the centre where they discussed what they had found. One 4 year old boy commented, "I didn't know we had so many mushrooms!"

The girl drew red and black mushroom shapes. She identified her black drawings as Shaggy Inkcap and her red drawings as Staghorn mushrooms by pointing to these on the ID chart. Looking at images depicting the different component parts of a mushroom, she drew another mushroom while identifying the roots and the cap on her picture.

A little boy commented, "Snails, fairies, beetles, worms … all eat mushrooms!"

Over the next few days, the children extended their play and learning with adult support by shaping a variety of fungi using clay and creating a mushroom garden in the woods.

Children in the centre have a good knowledge of fungi as they are fascinated by them and have a desire to find out more. This is a pattern that is repeated every year with children learning from each other, "Some mushrooms you can't eat, some you can.

Some can actually sting – small like leaves", "Only mushrooms at the shop you can eat", "Don't touch them!", "They poisoned ...like the Gruffalo's nose!"

The hazard of poisonous fungi is of concern to some of the staff and they did not feel that they have the knowledge yet to harvest mushrooms from the wild, to eat. The likelihood of a child becoming ill from touching the plants in the UK is remote, they would need to ingest a quantity for it to make them ill. One solution we are exploring is to introduce a 'mushroom log' to place in the vegetable area until the staff feel very confident. The parameters of this growing space ensure that the children know that plants here are safe to eat.

The children at a centre in Denmark work through an approach within a larger centre that has a focus on the methodology of delivery to a 'naturalistic' understanding of the world. In reality, this means that their routine is to leave the centre at 10 am to go to one of two sites to spend the rest of the day in an outdoor setting that has a shelter area. One of the features of the base room at the centre, is the presence and acceptance of the aspect of death in nature. There are displays of dead insects that have died or have been found as exoskeletons as creatures have grown. There were mole skins stretched on a frame as a traditional method of drying. The western eye would need to adjust to this display.

Death for many UK centres is spoken of but not displayed, the products from animals are hidden and not spoken of in an open way.

The process of hunting is accepted as part of the experience of living in this location. When the hunter comes to cull a chicken, they pluck and watch the 'drawing' of the offal and then cook the chicken over the fire to eat it.

Now, before some readers start to react, let us consider the options. There was a stage in England when practitioners thought it appropriate

to bring in real, dead fish to explore in a water tray. The fish were examined and then 'taken away'. Anders Farstad in Norway talks of catching fish and cooking it beside the lake on an open fire. Which do you feel gives a clearer picture? Is it as strange to let children know what they are eating, or should we be hiding and disguising 'food' in a mushy chicken nugget? We have chickens at the Nature Kindergartens. The conversations around their hatching have now morphed into questions about why some have long tail feathers and why there are no eggs. The point will come soon as to the fate of the cockerels. Do we take them

away? Cull them swiftly with those children who wish to see present? Do we share the full cycle of the food and cook it? Our decision is to a certain degree decided as we only provide vegetarian food which would make culling and eating a chicken an inappropriate option for the children we currently work with.

One day we found a hedgehog on the path that was dead. It's discovery lead to a conversation around its appearance, the permanence of death, the decay and heaven. The conversation those children had at that point will have prepared them in some way to the interpretation of death in other places, maybe a family member or a pet. There is a gravesite. We have moments of silence, burial services and celebrations of life for any living thing from flies, to the bird killed on the road. The garden has numerous sites. Their desire to dig up the hedgehog on the same day or a week later and then again months after was pure fascination from a group of boys. This record of conversation is in a Talking and Thinking Floorbook™, the reflection about the permanency of death, the final learning could not happen for a year when the bones were uncovered, this process of working in nature time is discussed more fully in

another chapter. Anyone who has grieved over a loved one will know how long the process takes, adults assume because children are visibly alright that the emotional acceptance is there. Only when the child talks and questions a year later do the adults start to realise the depth of thinking that can be internal, and that external dialogue is only applicable at certain times.

The Nature Kindergartens both have the wild woods and they give us the chance to happen upon the traces of death and decay. A deer skull, a dead bat, the remains of a foxes meal, are all there as a part of nature. Children find them fascinating, not horrific. They are as much of nature as a beautiful fragile butterfly.

The cycle of nature is that we enjoy the tiny lamb as cute, but are also aware of the size and strength as it grows, to its change into a sheep. Working with local farmers has allowed us to connect to community, so that all the children can experience the reality of nature. In Iceland, a traditional toy is made from a bag of sheep bones bleached and cleaned. The centres visited had trays as part of their construction zone, in their play the children used them very creatively. Across the other side of the world, in a Froebel inspired centre in Melbourne Australia, there were large skulls and jaw bones near to the block area, one could imagine life sized models being created

with amazing jaws and multiple heads. Is the use of bones appropriate, does it deepen understanding or extend the possibilities? If the answer is yes, perhaps adults should start to reflect on the degree of detachment we are often engaged in and start to see the use of materials as natural. We readily use feathers in the early years but purchase them in a way that has no connection to their origin, so we can forget the death of the bird when we use them. We even take away their natural beauty by dying them lurid colours.

Case study: 'Pheasant Death'

Children arrived at the centre one morning and found a dead pheasant outside. They were keen to take a closer look and a discussion ensued between the 2 to 4 year old children as to the cause of death. "It's cause something came to kill it, it was a tree wobbling and, and, the pheasant got killed!" "He got killed by hunters", " It was hit by a gun and fell on stones and was dead", "I

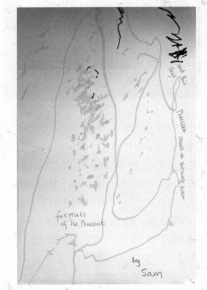

think Santa made him die cause he fell off his car", "I think he fell off the reindeer and hit on gravel", "Maybe a car drived over it?", "The car squashed him", "The hunters car drove over", " Why does it have closed eyes?" "Cause it bumped into a wall", "Maybe he bumped against a motorbike", "Maybe something squashed it with feet". A 4 year old boy commented, "I wonder if the pheasant bumped into electricity wires and he got electricity shock!"

The children expressed an interest in further investigating the dead pheasant and closely examined the eyes, the feathers and the feet. Some children wanted to see what was inside the pheasant and staff and parents supported the children keen to investigate this by dissecting the bird with the children. They closely examined the internal organs and one 4 year old boy was fascinated by the trachea and in a subsequent drawing commented, "I drew something inside the pheasant, it's like a worm with stripes on it". (see picture on the left).

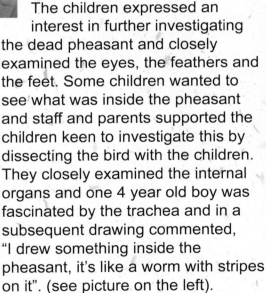

Back in the centre the children drew pictures of the pheasant, with many adding details such as feet, feathers and closed eyes.

The children went on to select a suitable place in the woods to bury the pheasant and after digging a hole they respectfully buried it. Children will still occasionally refer to the space where they buried the pheasant and wonder aloud when they will be able to dig up the bones to see the skeleton.

In role play children made pretend pheasant soup in a wheel barrow using water, mud and a big stick as a spoon measuring the soup with tape measures!

The experiences for many children in many parts of the world have become so removed from the interconnectedness of nature that they no longer perceive humans to be part of it. This separation has lead to both biophobia (fear of nature) and risk aversion. These aspects alone are beginning to affect the population as a whole, as the children born at the millennium are entering secondary education and in turn will soon be the voters of the future. If we as a society wish to preserve our planet first we need to understand it, we cannot do that if we have no connection to it. The deep level understanding is key to long term memory, even at a subconscious level the children have an internal map of emotions that they draw on when they meet new situations or have to make decisions.

Children in our centres are closely connected to nature and this includes the cycle of life and death. Cultures around the world have very different perceptions of death and the way that they feel it should be approached. It is taken as a given that each centre will be sensitive to all of these and treat people as individuals. From the experiences we have had, all children need to be supported through the process of bereavement, to try to find a place where it sits well with them, within their family and the wider community.

Key Points:

Children are connected to nature, we need to allow them to learn through real, meaningful experiences of it.

Adults working in a naturalistic space should be prepared to talk openly about all facets of nature that children encounter.

The rhythms of nature seem to trigger play behaviours and patterns in young children that adults need to be mindful of.

Chapter 15
A place to explore risk

'In nature there are neither rewards nor punishments; there are consequences'.

Robert Green Ingersoll

We need to ask ourselves a question: Do we really want to carry on the road of risk aversion that many societies around the world are on?

Risk taking should be part of childhood. We learn through the point where we feel challenged. The feeling of having a knot in your stomach is the place where you feel out of your comfort zone. As adults, the majority of us, do not put ourselves to a place where we are 'challenged', whether

emotionally, intellectually or physically. Emotionally, we surround ourselves with known social groups and if we were to place ourselves in a multiple daycare environment, and were required to meet so many new people everyday, we would probably not cope! Intellectually we pass through a threshold where at mid-teens or twenties, we move out of an academic situation into a place where applied skills and knowledge are more prevalent. The skills that we learn through risk taking are self confidence, emotional resilience, ability to self-risk assess situations synonymous with aptitudes in the adult world. There is a

current demand, or acceptance of ongoing development that requires practitioners to challenge themselves to reflect. For the children in our care, their rate and complexity of learning is something akin to speaking Shakespeare on a daily basis, so unless you are reading this in a theatre company, we need to reflect on our expectations of children so that we can see them as capable competent learners and not children to be wrapped in cotton wool across all areas of learning.

There are situations where nature has created a feeling of apprehension, it is a fear culture that is beginning to pervade all parts of the world where humans have lived in synergy with the local flora and fauna for hundreds of years. In our disconnection from the natural world, there has been an attempt to control nature, to create packaged experiences. This fear has been fuelled by some real restrictions and some misinterpreted boundaries that are imposed onto children's play. If children are the end stakeholders in the process, where are their voices about what they feel they need and want to do?

In the Nature Kindergartens the adult role is to remove hazards that children do not see, not the risk within the play. Deadwood from the tree canopy, unseen spikes of stick in jumping areas, venomous snakes behind rocks are removed, but it is not our role to remove challenge that children do see and then choose to undertake. Children can choose to climb up a tree and decide how far they feel comfortable climbing. If we remove all challenges children lose the feeling of aspiration which is so very important in terms of the drive to move forward in life. Children develop the ability to self risk assess as part of their learning. Our philosophy is to be hazard aware and not risk averse, and to employ a

sense of perspective when assessing play based situations. Children in the centre are aware of an indigenous plant called Stinging Nettles, their dangers, what they can be used for and the remedy for getting stung as the following conversation demonstrates:

"Nettles, do you know what's dangerous about nettles?" (Jago 4)

"They sting you, you know." (Caitlin 4)

"You can make soup with nettles. You need to put a glove on to pick them." (Donald 4)

"Rub ourselves with a dock leaf". (Caitlin 4)

Risk has a role to play in learning and, as research shows, has the potential to achieve positive outcomes for children. Children become strong stakeholders in their own development and show an increase in confidence and competence. They become independent and responsible for their own actions. They develop coping mechanisms, problem solving capabilities and transferable skills which also increases their self esteem and self belief. Children develop a respect for danger, hazards and experimentation. We can add to these potential outcomes by looking at the woodland environment - this natural environment is characterised by instability and this demands alertness by any user, regardless of their age (Nichols, 2000).

Offering children a risk-rich environment allows adults to help keep children safe by letting them take more risks, whilst guiding them through a progression of experiences. If risks are managed constructively during the play process, a 'child's desire to explore further' (O'Brien and Murray, 2006) can be fuelled. The best safety lies in learning how to deal with risk rather than avoiding it.

One of the key points to make here, is that safety is the responsibility of all of the staff and children. No one person could possibly take it all on board and be effective. Keeping yourself safe or, in a place where you feel safe, is an integral part of the process. Children are encouraged to be their own risk assessors and they are very good at it, if we give them the chance to learn through their own mistakes so that the boundaries are agreed and negotiated, rather than presented as set rules. This in itself is used as part of a good risk assessment.

The second key point is that if the adults do not read the benefit risk assessments created by others, and take note of their advice, then they are about as useful and relevant as a chocolate teapot!

In the Nature Kindergartens we offer and encourage 'risky play' with the adults there to scaffold the activity while the children gain confidence and become more competent both in self risk assessing and in mastering the activity. When discussing the possible risks of climbing trees Jacob (4) stated, "Only go as high as it doesn't scare you" while Francis (7) suggested, "If you can climb up a tree you need to be able to get down. Only go up as far as you feel safe". Practitioners trust children's decisions and believe that children have the right to choose to engage in challenge and test their developing skills. Benefit-risk assessments have to include all the stakeholders if they are to be effective.

Children in the Nature Kindergartens have access to a wide range of real tools, even children aged 2 years have access to tools such as junior hacksaws, hammers and so forth. They are able to choose the tools they would like to use from a Tree-Wrap™ suspended between the trees in the woods. Children also help to build fires and light them using a steel flint. The flint is much safer to use, since the process of developing the manual dexterity to use the flint evolves over time and supports the development of the understanding of the implications of lighting a fire. The adults are involved in the creation of policies and procedures, so that all staff have knowledge of the safe use of tools and lighting of fires.

Adults should not make a judgment about the hazards that may lead to a risk, without at the same time making a judgment about what benefits it might bring to children. For all the activities children need and want to undertake in our settings, we do a benefit-risk analysis where we do a comparison of the risk of a situation to its related benefits. 'Risk management that pursues only the objective of getting it wrong will be oblivious to significant opportunity costs' (Adams and Thompson, 2002).

Children seek challenge and in Denmark, they refer to that 'knot in the stomach' feeling as 'is i maven', which translates to 'ice in the stomach'. This is seen as a positive emotion and one that both children and adults seek. When the feeling of exhilaration becomes absolute fear then the experience often stops. Everyone has a different point where the one turns into another.

We believe that a benefit-risk assessment is not simply a technical matter but needs to be a value-based exercise which is dependent on the practitioner's knowledge about children's capacities, their resilience and their ability to make judgments. They also need to understand the benefits of at least some accidents and that some things can only be learnt through experience.

Case Study: 'The Climbing Frame'

The children at Auchlone Nature Kindergarten discovered a large, fallen tree and eagerly explored it. A child scratched herself on one of the sharp branches and the group decided that they needed to make the tree safe. They gathered and discussed the risks and then suggested ways of making the tree a safer place to play on. Tools were selected and children worked

together as a group using a variety of tools they had selected themselves. Some of the comments were "You can get bark in your eyes", "You might fall when the bark comes off, I need a metal hammer to break the loose bits", "I am getting all these bits off so children don't get splinters", "Is it safe to hold on? It is a bit wobbly", "This is a really sharp bit, pass me the mallet so I can chop it off". Most of the branches were cut to a metre length and then were measured by the children at the out of school club since they are the quality and standards team!

Visual triggers can be very useful for groups of children.

The groups agree a method whether it is red wire on a weak branch, or hazard tape on a pathway, the message system trusts children. The adult might reinforce the message but often the children instil the boundaries far more assertively than adults. Meetings, ideas and subsequent decisions are recorded by children in their Floorbook. The older group pointed out a hazard the younger children had not been aware of, a dead branch suspended in another tree above the space the children were working in! After a discussion, it was decided that the adult needed to climb up and tie a rope onto the branch and the children would work together to pull the dangerous branch off and away from the space. The children persevered at this task for nearly a week and at the end declared that they had created the best climbing frame ever!

Peter Heseltine of the Royal Society for the Prevention of Accidents, reflected on the move in the creation of playground spaces for children, "We have recommended the removal of anything dangerous, children are still getting hurt... We have forgotten why we have playgrounds, they are for children to play on... We have emasculated equipment. We inspect far more than necessary... We have covered everything in protective surfacing... We have made playgrounds so monumentally boring that any self respecting child will go somewhere else to play, somewhere more interesting and usually more dangerous. And quite right too..."

We are the people who need to decide what future we want our children to have, not a fearful agenda fuelled by litigation. Benefit risk assessments are empowering, they give us the confidence to be able to evidence that we have considered the hazards. There is a point where we have to consider that 'the real risk is ....that there is 'no risk' (Bundy, 2009).

Key Points:

Play without risk is not engaging and dynamic.

Being safe is about awareness and education not removal of hazards.

Benefit risk assessments are the responsibility of all stakeholders including children.

Chapter 16
A place to feel the dark

'In the right light, at the right time, everything is extraordinary'.

Aaron Rose

Nature Kindergartens and Forest Schools

The way that human beings have detached themselves from true darkness really interests me. There are few places in the UK that one can actually still experience real darkness. The people living in inner cities cannot see the stars. It is rare if you can see the stars and be able to see them all the way to the horizon. The feeling of who you are in a bigger frame, like the universe, is probably a discussion that all human beings have had. Young children have a natural connection to the bigger picture and are wonderfully simplistic of the larger questions we meet in life. Perhaps this comes down to the fact that they are always in a bigger frame than themselves and so to accept a stage beyond that to the universe, is an accepted framework.

The way we so often surround ourselves with artificial light all the time, has lead to a group of children who have no awareness of dark and have therefore, not developed, the ability to feel their way in the dark, or even to adjust their sight without a torch. Could this mean that the part

of the eye which is sensitive to darkness is probably less used than children fifty years ago? The fear of the dark comes from a wealth of different places, televisions that show things coming out of the dark, stories and tales that use the dark to add atmosphere because it feeds a fear set up by the withdrawal of one of the key senses, sight. Yet when we stay out in the dark we can see the subtlety of shade, of grey and black which gives a different feel to the same space. Moonlit nights are indeed magical, to see so clearly and yet without the traditional colour spectrum gives the natural world a new aspect. If darkness has such an effect on an adult, consider the impact of such a moment on a child.

The young children in our Nature Kindergartens have evenings when they are outside at dusk. In Scotland, we have a few days where we have some light for 24 hours in the height of our summer, conversely the darkness can be as long as 18 hours in the winter. In the deep winter it can be as early as three o'clock in the afternoon when the light starts to change. This gradual darkening is far less threatening than going from bright light into what people see as absolute dark. We encourage the children not to use torches all the time as they create areas of bright light against what appears to be dark areas. Our reliance upon electricity is very real when the battery in a torch is about to run out and you are in the woodland site. The sustainable aspect of our work is linked through everything we do, so wind-up lanterns, natural light, or home made

bees wax candles all feature in our work. On occasions, the wind-up torches have become part of an invented game of hiding. Reflective tabs and found materials to test as reflectors are hidden and have to be found by searchlight in the garden. During the darker evenings when the moon is away the children wear reflective safety jackets so that they flare up when the torch catches them.

A 4 year old boy shining his torch into a puddle; "It's got a reflection in the puddle, it's shining in it!"

A 4 year old boy, "Hey look, when I put the leaf on top it turns the light green!"

The experience children have with fire starts with candles. Candles are wonderful things. They offer so many ways for children to engage in exploration. The material they are made from, their shape and size, the smell they give out, the use of wax in creative projects, the power and heat they give off are all used

within the nature kindergarten. The indoor space is very natural, some say homely. The feeling people have when they walk in seems to be that of being rooted, welcomed. To look at how this is achieved, needs to focus on the detail the space affords. The links between experiences are carefully thought through, so the 'simple' actually belies complex consideration by the adult.

The table to eat from is set with a candle. Birthdays become a celebration of light as shown below. The subtlety of smell of the scent of rose, lavender or beeswax all add to the atmosphere

of the indoor space. The copper candle holders offer a fascination of reflection and over the years has been the provocation for many investigations into candle holders and how to 'make the light bigger' through reflective surfaces. Metal sculptures that move with the heat of a candle are used to give movement and also sound at key points in the year. Beeswax and mouldable wax are used in the creative zone. Molten wax is used by children and adults to create banners that have a wonderful translucent effect when the light highlights them. As the year changes in Scotland, and the daylight really draws in there is a large seasonal change for us in November through to February. Most countries around the world that have prolonged months of semi darkness have some festival of light, whether it is through the medium of ice in Alaska, or fires in Scotland, there is a link between humans and their need for light within the darkest months of the year. Candlelit jars and willow lanterns are used outside in the winter to highlight routes to the 'Light Tree'. The large sand area in the garden becomes a light sculpture in the winter with candles within small snow caves made by the children. The possible lines of development, experimentation and involvement with the children are outlined in the accompanying book entitled Journeys into Nature.

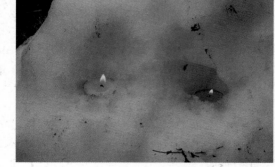

Fire is a wonderfully mesmeric light when it is used at night. The flames and colours become more intense. There are many occasions where I have sat in companionable silence with a group of children in the garden fire area, sharing some thinking time. Children need to feel ready to talk with subjects that are of relevance to them. Too often, the discussions meet adult agendas, with questions and subject matter identified by them. If we really want to raise oracy standards, then we need to offer experiences that are worthy of talk. A fire circle can often create an atmosphere for talk which indoor experiences fail to achieve.

The idea that the world does not stop when it gets dark or when children go to sleep is often at the root of many fears for children. That people work when you are asleep, that somewhere in the world it is daylight, that the sun will always rise is taken as a fact by adults. When young children were asked about the dark, their voices showed an understanding linked to received, second-hand experience from the television. The former is so powerful in terms of assimilation, that if we do not take children into the dark, they will continue with an unbalanced view. In order to explore the idea of the balance of night and day, a parent offered to set up an infrared web cam in response to their investigation of "Who comes in our wood when we go home?" The children have seen images of deer visiting their woodland site at night.

Stealth Cam 05-07-2008 10:53:30

Case Study: "In the Woods Tonight"

The children discovered an area in the woodlands that had been dug up overnight and found a small shallow tunnel. "Who made this hole, maybe a 'wee' mouse?" "I know mouses make holes cause they made a hole in my barn in the hay". The children agreed to come and revisit the space the next day to see if anything had changed.

The next day the children found the tunnel had been enlarged, this led to a discussion about who had come out to dig while the children were not in the woods, "A mouse", "Maybe a rat or a field mouse", " I think a rabbit 'cause rabbits dig tunnels under roots like this". The children had a lot of knowledge about the range of animals that could burrow and leave a tunnel such as the one they had found.

Over the next few days, the children continued to investigate the burrow site and commented on the changes they found, "Rabbits, no deer, a fox, I think a badger", were some of the responses.

Stealth Cam 09-19-2009 06:56:57

They knew that animals moved around the woods at night, having found evidence of activity and having seen deer on the stealth camera that had previously been placed in the woodlands overnight. The camera was again set up and when the film was analysed with the children, they identified a rabbit walking along the track towards the burrow. (see bottom left of image).

A member of staff was convinced that this was a badger burrow even with the evidence of the camera. One 4 year old girl offered a solution; "Maybe the rabbit is visiting the badger who made the hole!"

After this investigation the children did not revisit the burrow until weeks later, when they found that there was no evidence of any new digging and decided that the rabbit had moved out and found a better burrow.

Children are not born with a fear of dark, it develops over time. If they are with their peer group and a supportive adult, they are able to re-adjust their perceptions. If the parents and carers are also part of that process they can also see the beauty of the night, stars, moon scapes and moonfrost are far more subtle than the bright colours of day, and can be far more engaging. It does us good to realise that humans do not have a full dominance over nature, if we take away our artificial lighting we are on a more even level.

Key Points:

Humans are gradually being removed from the awareness of darkness, overlit areas are giving rise to large amounts of light pollution.

Candlelight and firelight have a mesmeric affect that can have a strong emotional connection to all humans.

Children should connect to their climate and seasons so that they understand the rhythm of them. Many children are unaware of nature's changes due to the amount of time spent indoors.

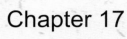

Chapter 17
A place where creativity is 'natural'

'Creativity is the power to connect the seemingly unconnected'.

William Plomer

What is creativity? Is it a creative table with art materials or perhaps outdoor transient art? Or is it in fact a way of thinking, looking for connections that build and create links and patterns in thinking? To my mind, it is the latter, too often the creative area is deemed to be the 'place' that 'it' happens.

The development of a creative play space inside and out is paramount in our work, if a child has the confidence to think, to enquire, to make links, to question, then they have the foundations for real learning for life.

Our whole approach leads us to this aspect. What we have discovered through watching children is that they use materials with high play affordance in a creative way. The materials that are there and that our climate provides are earth, wood, stone, water, wind, sky and light, vegetation, wool, blue flax and berries, the bountiful list can go on. In each climatic zone there is nature, although how it presents itself is very different. The Aeolian landscapes of dry desert have a stunning form, the constant shifting of sand, the subtle earth tones of places across the continent or down into the layers of the earth beneath in an outdoor zone are all nature, and all provocations for creativity.

Early experiences with the natural world have been positively linked with the development of imagination. The work of Edith Cobb (1977), is perhaps the most noteworthy in this regard. A large part of her work is based on a search for the creative principle in the human personality, involved a careful analysis of a wide variety of autobiographical recollections of highly creative adults. Many of these recollections reflected an 'early awareness of some primary relatedness to earth and universe'. Based on these and similar findings over her 20 years of research, Cobb concluded that childhood represents a special phase in life 'during which the most actively creative learning takes place'.

The ability for children to immerse themselves fully in their space, gives a freedom of thinking that allows a flow to take place. The connections run across areas defined by adults to make the learning holistic. Nature Kindergartens generally, but especially within the model of connection and extension into the wild woods are highly complex habitats offering children a multiplicity of encounters and sensations, a diversity of topography with all the colour, tone, texture, shape and pattern that we can imagine. There can be no other place that has such a profound effect on people as the natural world, and many of us see a very small part of it.

The garden areas are used partly as a sustainable source for the materials for the creative process. Willow beds, dogwood, contorted willow all provide long stems for constructing sculptures, shelters, and mobiles. The plants give us a dye source for fabrics and wool, they give us materials to plait, twist and shape, the earth gives us materials to sieve in order to make a fine mouldable clay or to grind down to give us mud paint, the animals give us wool and beeswax, the sky sometimes gives us sun, or shadows and always gives us cloud shapes to watch, water gives us the ultimate transferable liquid, changing form as the seasons move on through the year. Each of these materials warrants time. Time to really explore their potential and explore the epistemic nature of them, before necessarily using them for a set purpose.

It is at this point that the consultative strategies held within the Floorbooks feature in our work, these may focus entirely on investigations into mud, on ice, on a plant, not the whole plant kingdom, just one. The creativity comes from standing back to really see, or perhaps it is standing close to connect to the material you are using. The activity driven programmes of some early years spaces, whether forest schools or not, must stifle the investigative process. The flow through the creation of the clay from fine loam soil with water, to how it dries and separates, to how it absorbs water to a point where it flows away again. Then the investigation goes into the flow of mud slips, mud slides to dams and blocks, to tributaries, then to the formation of a lake. The interest went to explore the malleability of the material as you can see in the case study at the end of the chapter. The change is in the adult mindfulness, that they are present but patient. Not hurrying children to get to the next thing because the adult has done it a thousand times before.

The adult needs some knowledge to consider what lies behind the materials and how to get the best out of them. Fisher (2005), supports this when he states, 'children learn best when they have access to the generative power of those around them'. The skills are in the background, to enable the adult not to empower them to take over the experience. There is a plan afoot to put a Raku kiln at one of the centres, as well as a traditional electric one in a nearby training centre. When we evaluate how connected the children can be, the Raku pottery experience would be far more inclusive since the children can create the hole, gather the wood and set the kiln to fire their own clay work, only stepping back at the firing point.

Early experiences with the natural world have been positively linked with the sense of wonder. Wonder, as described by Cobb (1977), is not an abstract term or a lofty ideal. It is, instead, 'a phenomenon concretely rooted in the child's developing perceptual capabilities and his or her ways of knowing. This way of knowing, if recognised and honored, can serve as a life-long source of joy and enrichment, as well as an impetus, or motivation, for further learning', (Carson, 1956). Edith Cobb (1977), who concluded from her research that 'experience in childhood is never formal or abstract. Even the world of nature', she says, 'is not a 'scene,' or even a landscape. Nature for the child is sheer sensory experience'.

I come back here to Joseph Clinton Pearce (1977), and his discussion of the primary perceptions of a child, using the term 'magical thinking' to describe the child's way of knowing the world. These primary perceptions, Pearce notes, 'are developmental in that they tend to disappear'. Pearce describes these primary perceptions as 'bondings to the earth' and suggests that interaction with the physical substance of the living earth, for example rocks, trees, wind is critical to the child's developing brain and intelligence.

Building with clay is traditional in Scotland. Celtic roundhouses (stone and clay circle with timber roof), round houses (with a hole in the roof), Cob huts (where the clay is harden and burnished to make it semi permeable) can be built in large size or as fairy dens. On a recent trip to work in New Zealand we made fine clay to create a fairy village on the side of a hill. The process of creating the clay was all absorbing, each adult group creating a different blend, considering how to mix and perfect the consistency. Large pod cases were the mixing bowls and each group considered the options of cohesion to get the 'best' clay. The task was to explore fire hazards and safety, as well as creativity, since the tealight inside was lit as dusk came. The shapes for basic dwellings and houses around the world are in fact, similar because of the type of materials used for construction.

There are so many case studies that we could have put into this chapter, but we have chosen to share a learning story about mud in a Nature Kindergarten in Scotland and one in South Africa. They show that there is a core connection to the earth when the children are outside for long blocks of time, and their learning transcends the geographical areas to link children around the globe.

Case study: 'Mud, Sand and Water'

In Scotland the children in both of our centres regularly explore and use mud as a creative media. We have found that children of different ages throughout the world also choose to use this versatile malleable material.

At Whistlebrae, children aged 2 to 5 years placed white sand onto a willow structure pressing it into the willow weave to make it adhere. "This is our beehive and the bees go through that hole, they make honey".

A child added a few drops of mud using her fingers and commented on the contrast between the white sand and the dark mud. "This is a house for the fairies, they fly through this hole and go inside".

Children added leaves to decorate the structure and soon the mud replaced the sand. Mud of a thicker consistency was mixed to block off the central hole and children watched as the mud repeatedly fell into the gap.

A 2 year old boy collected the mud and formed the mud into little balls on a slice of wood, "Cakes, this is sugar, icing sugar, my mummy decorates mine with icing sugar", as he sprinkled white sand onto the mud balls. Leaves of different colours were added. Cups of water were poured over the structure which washed the remaining white sand away, "Making a waterfall".

A 4 year old boy selected the longest pieces of grass he could find and carefully placed them around the gap, "I am making a window, a square window for the fairies". More grass and leaves were added. One 4 year old boy added a rope through the gap, "This is a fairy house and a beehive. The bees fly in the top and the fairies in the door. When you pull the rope like this, the bees sit on the rope and hold on and come out so they don't need to fly!"

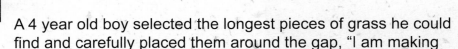

At Auchlone a 4 year old boy used his hands to shape mud onto a wooden slice, "A mudmonster, a scary mudmonster". He looked around him and added a variety of natural and found objects to add detail to his monster. His peers joined in and brought objects with ideas on what they could represent, "A nose, a long pointy one", "This could be the arm, no hand, it doesn't have arms". The boy accepted or rejected suggestions, manipulating and moulding the mud and objects to create a transformational object. The boy added a sphere, "Eye, only one, this is a one eyed mud monster!"

In South Africa, a group of boys were collecting mud from a dam and shaping this into a variety of shapes. One 5 year old boy created a small ball in the palm of his hand and then using his thumb, he made an indent into the ball to form a small bowl, "Now I will leave this in the hot sun and it will get dry and very, very hard and then it will turn into a rock!"

Another group of boys aged 6 to 7 years moved closer to the water to find mud of a different consistency and spread the clay mud around a ball, they talked about the perfect texture and consistency needed to create a mud football. The boys spent a long time creating the covering for their mud ball and then placed this into the sun to dry. When the mud dried, the little bowl was rock hard and could hold a small amount of water while the mud around the ball cracked and flaked off the plastic when the boys tested their mud football!

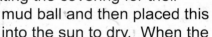
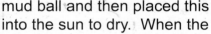
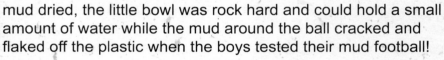

Creativity is a way of thinking, an approach of discovery, full of questions, decisions and ideas that circulate constantly, until at points, there may seem to be a point of conclusion. Children spend a great deal of time processing rather than reaching the points of conclusion.

Key points:

Creativity is an approach to learning, that is cross curricular.

Early experiences of the natural world have been positively linked with the development of imagination.

Appropriate naturalistic spaces, both inside and out support children to be free to engage fully and deeply in their thinking without interruption.

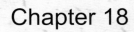

Chapter 18

A place that is the 'environment' in every aspect.

'Take nothing but pictures. Leave nothing but footprints. Kill nothing but time'.

unknown

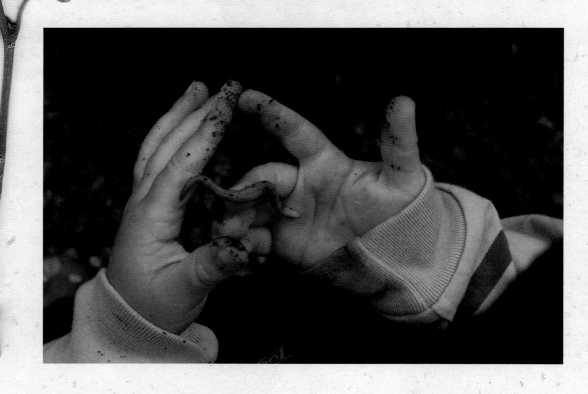

The environment is under pressure. The majority of human beings, thankfully, are becoming more aware that they need to start living in a way that links them to nature through a desire to minimise their 'footprint' whether carbon or literally onto the space around them. There are a number of environmental approaches across the planet that work with children. The Eco Schools programme, the enviro-schools of New Zealand, the Green schools of Iceland all of these and many more not listed here, are moving along to try to raise awareness of global issues and how society can all make a difference. It is of interest that people talk of dealing with the environment rather than seeing that they are intrinsically connected to it. The day to day living in the Nature Kindergartens focuses on waste minimisation, litter management systems, low energy use, outdoor spaces, sustainability (global perspectives), healthy eating, biodiversity, and educational grounds. In our approach, we also operate sustainably through ethical trade, we source organic solutions, and commit ourselves as a group to all the small actions detailed in this book that can then combine to create the vision.

There will always be a balance between nature education and conservation. Children need to connect to the world around them if they are going to be motivated to conserve it. The way that children connect to nature at different stages in their lives will undoubtedly alter. The benefit of working with children from one year old, is that nature becomes the core of their learning environment. The sensorial development of children is developed by all aspects of being outside in a naturalistic play space (Warden 2005). Many parents choose a Nature Kindergarten because they had an experience of picking daisies or making mud soup, their understanding comes from using the environment for play and the emotions it created. In the project work we do in challenging spaces with parents with a low self esteem, it is apparent that there is little or no memory retained of connecting to the outdoor environment. For these adults their awareness and support of conservation draws on extrinsic sources rather than intrinisic motivation and as such they feel little connection to nature and are often more focussed on the lunch break or the free resource. It is hoped through working with these groups that they will 'feel' something that can be used as a starting point for further development.

The impact of groups accessing natural spaces is not without it's challenges. The areas are fragile in terms of their diversity and can be completely changed following human contact. Moss can only be trodden on four times before it dies, in fact one of the current ways of controlling bracken is to bruise it by treading on it in its early form. If we look at the individual footprint and then multiply it up for a group it is obvious that we need to look at the site management so that areas of heavy use are given respite to re-grow and adapt.

There has been a balance to explore between the introduction of our Nature Kindergarten approach and access to countryside and the preservation of the fragile habitats anywhere, whether on a beach or in a forest, the natural spaces all need to be cared for and to a certain degree protected. One of the elements of working in a wild space is to create a management plan of how the site will be used to minimise the impact. In places where there are hundreds of acres, it is easy to take a journey to a different location to change the route to minimise the impact. In smaller spaces, the impact becomes very evident and in some cases does require careful management. If you go into most national parks in the UK, there will be a designated pathway to focus erosion into smaller areas, thereby leaving other areas untouched. There are areas of wildness in the garden spaces of the Nature Kindergartens, created by child-made fencing.

There has had to be some action taken in the areas immediately outside the lodges, where the rain has been extreme and therefore, the ground has become waterlogged. We use hay on top of the grass to protect it from the extreme use of active children. The grass grows through the mesh effectively, stimulated by the light. Covering areas in bark will serve to block out light and therefore, make more defined paths rather than encourage the grass to grow. The children have become the guardians of the space and will often get out some rods and hazard tape to mark out areas that require children to be gentle.

At Auchlone Kindergarten, the children have pathways that ebb and flow – I mentioned them earlier. This approach minimizes their impact on one section and allows the ground to 'recover' in the hardest months of the year. The lines for the pathways are defined by the children who position the rope to show the lawnmower where to go. The woodland spaces provide more opportunity to spread their impact, but there are still fragile flora and fauna that cannot withstand too much handling. In order to define these spaces, children create lookout signs that are designed, made and installed by them. Given the age of the children, we do not use traditional environmental games that were defined by people such as Joseph Cornell. The belief that children will love nature, and protect what they love, has been very effective since most children operate in a way that is emotive and responsive.

Many centres have written rules about picking wild flowers for obvious reasons, however as a play area for two to six year olds, the most popular activity is to make petal perfume. The idea that a rare orchid could be destroyed is indeed worrying, but is the long term gain of picking a daisy to explore its beauty not greater than the short term loss? Nature will 'cycle round' to produce more flowers sometimes within a few days. Knowledge has to be the key, to create informed populations of children and adults so that unconscious incompetence is limited. A survey of the plants on site may highlight the need for more prolific plants that can be gathered. It may also provocate a conservation and protection habit as seen at Auchlone when the aconites came up.

The children in the Nature Kindergartens are empowered by their knowledge, not necessarily of the nomenclature but of the behaviour of the flora and fauna. The knowledge has to be about the world around them since they are connected to it, the 'knowledge' or perhaps 'wisdom' will affect nature on both urban and rural sites far beyond the confines of their own wild space.

In some of the more challenging spaces that I work, the effect of opening up of small woodland sites has also raised the awareness in communities of vandals, who systematically destroy a space that could in fact offer them much of what they seek. Groups have sought out community links that have not existed before as community woodlands are cared for and managed, the use of these spaces has been positive both for the children and the wider groups that support them.

In the Nature Kindergartens, the culture we try to develop is of one of guardianship of the natural spaces and as such there is a residual knowledge of the natural world. In this country we have knowledge but it often lies in the hands of specialist rangers who are removed from the classroom (and are therefore viewed as a bolt on opportunity). For the forest to become a teaching space, we need to place the knowledge of how to use the natural world around the schools and centres in the hands of the teachers and educators so that it becomes embedded in the day to day teaching of the school.

When the site is used for Forest School, the effect of transporting children is always of high concern given the amount of emissions. Living in a rural community, it does make you far more aware of driving to get what you need. Without transportation we limit the children having access to very small numbers with local communities and one could argue that these are the very children that need a connection to nature. Ultimately, it would be wonderful to have nature spaces or forest schools within reach of all schools. Indeed Oxfordshire County Council has created a planning outline which supports new build centres being within 15 minutes of a forest site, but for many regions in the U.K., this is still a distance away.

The environment, both inside and out, is cared for by the children at the Nature Kindergartens in a practical way. The eco-schools programme is a performance indicator within the evaluative self assessment programme present in educational establishments. The programme is linked to the categories listed as waste minimisation, management, healthy eating, energy use, biodiversity and sustainability.

There are water collection butts for play, grey water management for watering plants, recycling bins, composters, solar panels and many sustainable materials grown to use within the experiences in the kindergarten. Many of the systems such as the wormery, were designed by the children and are created out of natural materials in the wood. The children's focus changes and all things morph into others due to the nature of the materials, they went back into the earth where they had come from, with no visible impact.

In some instances, the materials have been collected from a range of areas to minimize the wild habitat change and used within the garden areas. The wild pond and habitat 'basket' made at the Nature Kindergarten were put in to increase the biodiversity of the space. The fence and their gateway were created by the children to raise awareness and sensitivity to the protection of the space.

In summary, enabling people to access flora and fauna will undoubtedly incur some damage. The benefit is a heightened awareness and knowledge that can be used in a positive way, if they have a deeper emotional connection to the environment and an intrinsic motivation to conserve it.

Ecologists, environmental psychologists, and others suggest that we all have a natural attraction, or affinity, for life (Kaplan & Kaplan, 1989; Orr, 1994). This affinity for life has been referred to by E.O. Wilson (1984, 1992), as biophilia, such as a love of nature. If this natural attraction is not encouraged or given opportunities to flourish during the early years of life, the opposite, biophobia (i.e., an aversion to nature), may occur. Orr (1994) goes on to suggest that 'Biophobia ranges from discomfort in 'natural' places to active scorn for whatever is not manmade, managed, or air-conditioned'.

Biophobia is also manifested in the tendency to 'regard nature 'objectively' as nothing more than 'resources' to be used'" (Orr, 1994). There is a tendancy for this approach to be adopted as mentioned earlier of canned nature, presented to children rather than being found by them. Disregarding young children's ways of knowing and pushing them to early abstractions about the natural world for example, cognitive models that may lead to biophobia at the expense of biophilia. The balance of emotional exploration versus intellectual tasks has been a balance for many nature based programmes. The cognitive models are however, much simpler to assess and process data, which means that projects that look at impact may resort to avoiding the affective domain. Experiences during the early childhood years give form to the values, attitudes, and basic orientation toward the world that individuals carry with them throughout their life (Wilson, 1994a). Thus, it is not surprising that early positive experiences with the natural environment have been identified repeatedly as one of the 'significant life experiences' associated with responsible environmental behaviour (Chawla & Hart, 1988) and the development of biophilia. 'If by some fairly young age... nature has not been experienced as a friendly place of adventure and excitement, biophilia will not take hold as it might have'. (Orr, 1994).

Case Study: 'Our Wildlife'

As part of our eco schools project a commercial wormery was ordered, delivered and children helped to set it up. They looked at the number of worms released, "1,2,3 they're wiggling", "They're all tied up, they knotted!" One 4 year old boy examined and 'tickled' the worms escaping through the narrow holes of the wormery.

In the woodland, the children found more earthworms and wanted to bring these down to the garden space and include them into the wormery; "A giant worm, I found a giant worm!" "I can see blood – there in its body", "It just slides up", "It

pushes its body", "Earthworms don't have legs, they just wiggle". Children focussed on the movement of the

earthworm for half an hour and watched it 'climb' up an embankment. After discussion about biodiversity the children agreed that it would be better to leave the earthworms in the woods and create a special woodland wormery for them. They designed and then created their own wormery, "This is the wall so they know where their house is", "That says 100,000 that means 100,000 worms can be in our wormery!"

This interest in the preservation of nature continued and children were keen to create other habitats within the centre.

One 4 year old girl commented that she had not seen any toads for a while and the discussion became one of how they could encourage wildlife back into the garden space, "A toad garden where people don't walk", "Some of those purple flowers for butterflies", were some of the suggestions.

The children all worked together to design and then create an area in the garden that would encourage and allow wildlife to thrive. They decided that a barrier was needed to define where people walked freely and what was to become the space

for the toads. A fence was built "With windows so we can see inside", "A gate so you can go in but not all the time".

Using an old basket children added sticks, bamboo bits and other vegetation to create a suitable habitat for small animals and bugs.

The basket became the focal point for many weeks. Children selected 'special sticks' and 'yummy food' that they felt a toad would adore. Appropriate tools such as loppers and secateurs were used to cut up the materials so that they would fit inside the basket. The mathematical concepts were as high on the agenda for the children as the environment they were creating. Children cut up sticks to exact dimensions such as a centimetres, or the size of a 'lolly stick' to fill all the gaps in the basket. As the contents started to rot each subsequent group of children added their 'yummy food' to the mix.

The children were rewarded when they spotted the first toad in their enclosure and soon the tadpoles in the pond area turned into tiny frogs children could observe on a daily basis. Within a short time, lacewings and butterflies appeared in the wild flower area and when the children spotted little field mice in the stone walls, they agreed that now the animals were all back in their garden space.

The balance of access and protection is always a struggle when moving out to start new programmes. The Floorbook, will be the process that can evidence children's growing awareness of the environment and how we can care for it. Future groups can then take forward the ideas over a number of years for long term change.

Key points:

The emotional connection to the planet at a young age may well be the foundation for the love and protection of the earth at a later stage in life.

The balance of impact on the environment can be explored through child designed programmes such as fence building.

The balance of knowledge and emotion about the natural world needs to be balanced at the early stages of exploration.

Chapter 19

Sustainability of the approach

'You have to leave the city of your comfort and go into the wilderness of your intuition. What you'll discover will be wonderful. What you'll discover is your own beliefs'.

Alan Alda

One of the more troubling pieces of research explored by Kahn (2002), is the notion of 'environmental intergenerational amnesia', the notion that each generation takes the state of the environment that they experience, as the norm. This means that each generation is only disturbed by significant changes in their life time and not the long term trends over generations. How do we challenge that concept as a society today? How do we as educators offer a different perspective to challenge norms? It is difficult to talk about duration of time and global issues with very young children. However, we can as adults take on the decisions that will enable our children to love and understand the natural world around them. Not through second hand experiences in a book, or television but through being outside in nature for long, experiential blocks of time, so that they have memory and emotion to draw on in later life.

This Chapter will explore the transferability of the Nature Kindergarten approach as it has been defined in this book to spaces in varying climatic and cultural zones. To areas where people are trying to support a child' s right to be outside before that also becomes a cultural norm in the world.

Nabhan and Trimble (1994), maintain that middle childhood from around 7 years old to puberty, is a period where children's brains are physiologically well developed but they do not yet take on adult roles. This period is full of potential for playing, imagining, creating and receiving, when children are 'in love with the universe' (Cobb1977). If it is as Nabhan and Trimble suggest then we should be looking not to the age of 5 but onto the age 7-11 years and beyond as the next commitment for naturalistic spaces. How wonderful it would be to create spaces for children in the first stage of their experiences of the educational system that support their 'love for the universe'. In Scotland we have a curriculum for excellence that is supporting this active approach to learning, but only a few schools have truly embraced the outdoor access for children up to 11 years. In the English and Welsh foundation stage there is now a acceptance that children to the age of 7 should have access to outdoor learning.

I am delighted to see pockets of innovative practice, stimulated by our work such as a childminder in Fife, an outdoor nursery in Glasgow, or education authorities using the Floorbooks to consult children across the country. There are a rising number of innovative rural primary schools sharing their nature based, outdoor practice such as Inverary in Argyll and Bute. All the people involved have come to see natural spaces, through evocative qualities of mystery and magic, these qualities feed children's sense of wonder and provide plentiful imaginative and creative play affordances (Moore and Wong 1997). The challenge we have is to transfer these elements to spaces that are in challenging zones such as those with high vandalism, hard spaces or risk averse methodologies and to sustain the elements throughout a child's school life.

It is with this goal in mind, that our work is more focussed on urbanised areas, whether through a shorter session of forest school experience or in a true Nature Kindergarten experience, all day, every day.

The durability of our approach relies on the way it can be integrated into other environments, beyond the Scottish Curriculum into other curricula and physically away from the rural space we work in, to urban environments and from one country and culture to another. Here are three case studies to look at the development of Mindstretchers style of Nature Kindergarten. As people share their stories with us, we in turn share them with you in the hope that they offer motivation for change.

Application of the methodology in an urban area in the South of England

Whilst travelling across the UK to facilitate training on the approach I met the enthusiastic members of Rainbow Pre-school. The pre-school operates within a porta cabin (fondly referred to as the green hut) in a residential area. The children range from 2 to 4 years old. The playroom has access onto an outdoor area. The site did have a decking area, but was used very rarely and often used for physical opportunities that were stimulated by plastic fixed equipment. The journey to use Floorbooks had begun, but only 3 weeks before a visit by Ofsted inspectors who look at the quality of provision. In 2006, a group of practitioners travelled up from the South of England to experience the Nature Kindergarten at Whistlebrae in Scotland. The environment was free of children so adults could sit, settle, play, explore and reflect on their own space and consider the effect of the environment on the way they were feeling and thinking. Training about the methodology was part of the experience so that the ideas could come together as an integrated learning experience. The floorbooks shared the personality and ethos of the individual Nature Kindergarten, so that discussions and reflections could happen in relation to the role of the adult in a child's learning journey. The skill of listening to children and considering how much to record was discussed as a group. The purpose for the floorbooks is to elevate children's ideas through talk and more widespread forms of communication. Some of their purpose is to provide research for adults to reflect on their practice, and how they can understand how children learn. Rainbow pre-school had two aspects to explore both a naturalistic outdoor area and the development of a consultative method of planning.

The first part of any change process is the acknowledgement that there is a need for change and then a way of defining where the journey should go, and how the journey will unfold. Support from the local authority had suggested that it would be good to be out more often and that children should be at the base of planning. The Floorbooks came in as a record of conversations, full of ideas that surprised the adults who had been very involved in the decision making for the planning. The children created characters and offered ideas for design of the spaces, both inside and out.

The determination of the staff to move towards a position closer to a Nature Kindergarten was very high. An area of decking had been built up to a point that enabled children to walk straight out onto the deck, to avoid the use of steps. The decking was taken up to reveal a larger, lower area with several trees. Concepts of freedom, empowerment and sensorial development were discussed and therefore, naturally emerged from the children as nature began

to reconnect them. Children started to ask to be outside, staff started 'to become one with nature'. All members of the community were involved from aunts to grandparents, local builders gave up their 'waste' materials which were then given another life in the landscape of the outdoor area and old plastic equipment was given away.

The centre of the space used the old sand area and hid the plastic elements to create a visually calmer space. The box also doubled as an elevated area, with a small step to encourage children up. This gave children a different perspective of their area. The staff response to the elevation was to be calm about risk of falls and through the process of risk assessment identify that a key part is to discuss with children issues around safe climbing and leaping. Having explored the idea of elevation they then looked at dens and hiding spaces. A corner that had been unused was covered in with the old decking to create a den to hide in. Simple use of recycled materials had been used by the children to decorate the inside, so they obviously had a real sense of place, many stories and chats had obviously taken place since the children were comfortable in the space.

The vertical surfaces of fence were covered in materials such as bamboo guttering that was then used through a series of metal loops to create a balance and pivot system. Children were then able to take loose materials such as pebbles, wood, sand and create barriers and objects to roll down the slopes. An old tyre was used to create a small grit pit. The variety of materials is part of the sensorial development of the children, so more smaller containers with a greater variety is better for challenging play in a small area than one medium sand pit that is never altered. Children were encouraged to explore produce such as tomatoes and potatoes so that they could experience harvesting rather than simply growing. Many small areas do miss the potential of harvesting, whether it is gathering seeds to replant, flowers to actually use, seed pods to explore or fruit and vegetables to consume. The children go out of their area to their 'wild wood' as often as they can. Rainbow pre school showed others that it does not require a great deal of space, but it does require a change of mindset. The continuum is endless and the next steps will be the space of the indoor environment, as the effect of nature takes hold, so the indoor space starts to morph to become gentler and more visually simple.

Application of the methodology to the cultural ethos of New Zealand.

In a presentation at the World forum in 2007, and again at a Childspace conference in Wellington, I met Cherry, a very enthusiastic early educator based in Whangerei in the Northland area of New Zealand. A year later, I was presenting to a large group of practitioners in her locality in the north island, New Zealand. At that session, were all the staff who worked at Open Spaces, a childcare centre, (6 months to 4yrs) set amongst stone walls, beautiful fields and mature forests. In 2009, a three day outdoor conference was set in the 'wild woods', to explore

the development of Nature Kindergartens in New Zealand. Individuals have a belief in nature and our connection to it, but the time seems to be right now to create a more solid framework of commitment. The Maori culture is so well embedded in New Zealand that it was very evident that the connection to the land could be linked in to everyday experiences of children in a meaningful way. The group of enthusiasts set up an independent body under the name of Natural Phenomena to promote the development of nature based learning such as Forest School and Nature Kindergartens. The team at Open Spaces, began to create a 'wild wood' based on the model seen at Auchlone and Whistlebrae in Scotland in an area of land about 10 minutes walk from the centre.

The New Zealand curriculum, 'Te Whāriki' is well known around the world, but as with all change of governments, the dilemma of consistency and changing regulations of assessment and monitoring can be at odds with the values set out by previous groups. Through all the changes in government and policy, run children's natural behaviours. They are in many ways similar around the globe and that should be our constant guide. The children go to the wild woods three times a week, they have special climbing trees, bouncing woods and rock mountains. The space

has some adult creations, a stage made of rock and turf, a fairy knoll, a stone and wooden hut,

a fire pit and a provocation of a woven wall with bamboo. The area has deer, pigs, sheep and horses that children are encouraged to care for by the provision of food and water.

The land 'Whenua', is fundamental to Maori identity, as it embodies the path and the foundations for future generations (Williams 2004). Maori believe that every living thing is connected and as humans on the earth, we have a role to play in nurturing 'Mauri' Mana. The guardianship 'Kaitiakitanga' of the sky, the sea and the

land became an area that the adults wanted to develop and extend in the Nature Kindergarten, inside and outside, but especially in the way the children 'are' in the wild woods. It is important that Maori and non-Maori come together to reflect on the notion of kinship with nature, and how this idea might be useful in an environmentally threatened world.

In July 2009, the staff, Barbara and Clayanne, brought together these thoughts on their journey so far (taken from learning story). The challenges in applying 'Kaitiakitanga' is the need to understand traditional concepts such as 'mana' (status), 'tapu' (spiritual restrictions) and 'mauri' (life principles) and relate them to the modern setting.

How were we kaitiaki (caring) today? The children greatly enjoy the variety of trees available to climb and play in the wild wood. The Totara are particularly strong and have a lot of branches to climb. I did climb the tree to test its strength and safety for the children. A little girl started to worry about me climbing, so I came back down. This area of the wood has mana with abundant tree growth. On this day, I stopped and showed children the prolific (maapua) regeneration of 'nikau' in different areas. There are only a few of these beautiful trees in the paddock, yet many seedlings. The children found a spider and carefully put it on the branch in the wood hut so the 'pungawerewere' could play with him. The children are careful of the creatures in this space, replacing rocks and carefully returning animals to their homes.

Some children have made some three dimensional art in the forest. We talked about their desire to take them home. Should they stay in the forest? Should we take from the space we are in? We sometimes gather different resources and taong for the use at the centre. These resources and taonga are only gathered if we need them. In this way the children and staff are respecting and supporting the growth of Papatunauku and Taane Mahuta's mauri.

When we stopped for lunch we sang our 'whakakapai kai'. At first the children sang in a silly way, we were silent and listened to the sounds of nature around us. Then, one little girl sang on her own and we listened with respect. We gathered our food scraps to share with the animals on the way back to the centre. As 'nga kaitiaki' (guardians) of the wild woods, we are sure to respect the place by looking after it. All the equipment that is taken to the 'wild woods' is taken

back to the centre, if we need it in the day it is stored for us in a hollow tree. We respect the way the area is naturally formed and don't interfere with how it is laid out, creating a mutual bond between children, staff, Papaptunaku and Taane Mahuta.

The 'wild space' at Open spaces has a sense of gravitas, it is a space that is

used now but looked after for the future generations to come.

The next step is to deepen the knowledge and skills of the staff to acknowledge their thinking and reflection. It may lead to a further nature based qualification, it may just lead into a deeper understanding of global research and what it means for the staff and children in New Zealand. This will affect both the staff confidence, the parent's perception of the importance of the wild wood and the support of the registration body that affects many aspects of education. In 2010, there will be another event with some in-depth training in the forest, at the 'wild woods'. The story continues.

Application of the methodology to a different climatic zone in Australia

For those of us who live in countries that have no poisonous insects or reptiles, where

temperatures are always temperate, the stereotypical image of Australia is one that evokes high temperatures, and risk assessments that would create a book! This case study shares some images from a wonderful space in Eastern Australia.

I have been motivated by the connection I have with Kirsty who works at St Leonard's College near Melbourne in Australia. We have now shared our work through exchange visits. In 2009, I was invited to visit their new wild wood that

was created after a visit to Auchlone Nature Kindergarten in Scotland. The grounds of the school reflect the close connection the whole school places on nature and their care of the planet. New orchards have been planted, chickens kept and a small vineyard was underway. The space around the school offers children a sense of freedom. The awareness of the hazard of bush fire was explored through displays that shared children's fears and thinking. Parents and carers were fully involved in thinking through the process surrounding the children's need to connect to nature, puddles were explored, discussions surrounding hazards such as muddy slopes were all valued in displays and in link books

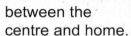

between the centre and home.

The early years area already had the ethos of naturalistic learning inside and had a beautiful naturalistic space for their children outside so the final aspect was to explore the essence of the wild areas.

The children wear sun hats and carry water. Everyone wears wellington boots to minimise the risk of snake bites, their personal knowledge to stay out of long grass, to avoid feeling around rocks, or to always look behind before you reach was very evident as they guided me past the 'Guardian dragon' and on into the wild space to reach the camp. Children were given space to choose a pathway, sometimes over a bridge and sometimes through the gulley.

The base camp had a simple shelter next to the fire area which was defined by an edging area to prevent fire 'creep' underground. The choice of site opposite gave children the shade they needed, water was close by for both learning and also for the fire buckets. The parents came on the trip to be with us in the space, so children from 6 months old were part of the community. The experiences and reception that the work on our approach to Nature Kindergartens has had across the world, gives me great hope that early educators are becoming more aware of how to live and be sustainable in all that we do. It gives me great heart that people are moving along a similar route to enable all children to connect to nature, wherever they are.

Bibliography.

Adams, E. (1991). Back to basics: Aesthetic experience. *Children's Environments Quarterly, 8*(2), 19-29.

Adams, J., & Thompson, M. (2002). Taking account of societal concerns about risk: framing the problem. *Health and Safety Executive. Research Report,* 35.

Barnes, P., & Sharp, B. (Eds.). (2004). *The RHP companion to outdoor education.* Dorset: Russell House Publishing.

Bialik, H. N. (1939). *Aftergrowth, and other stories.* Philadelphia: The Jewish publication society of America.

Bixler, R. D., Floyd, M. F., & Hammitt, W. E. (2002). Environmental Socialization: Qualitative Tests of the Childhood Play Hypothesis. *Environment and Behavior, 34*(6), 795-818. doi: 10.1177/001391602237248

Bodkin, F., & Robertson, L. (2008). *Dharawal: Seasons and Climatic Cycles:* F. Bodkin & L. Robertson.

Bonel, P., & Lindon, J. (2000). *Playwork: A guide to good practice:* Nelson Thornes.

Borradaile, L. (2006). Forest School Scotland An Evaluation: Foresty Commission Scotland.

Bronfenbrenner, U. (1990). Discovering what families do. In D. Blankenhorn, S. Bayme & J. Elshtain. (Eds.), *Rebuilding the Nest: A New Commitment to the American Family* (Vol. 6, pp. 07).

Bundy, A. C., Luckett, T., Tranter, P. J., Naughton, G. A., Wyver, S. R., Ragen, J., & Spies, G. (2009). The risk is that there is 'no risk': a simple, innovative intervention to increase children's activity levels. *International Journal of Early Years Education, 17*(1), 33-45.

Carson, R. (1988). *The sense of wonder.* New York: Harper & Row.

Chawla, L. (1990). Ecstatic places. *Children's Environments Quarterly, 7*(4).

Chawla, L. (2002). Spots of time: Manifold ways of being in nature in childhood. In P. Kahn & K. S. (Eds.), *Children and nature: Psychological, sociocultural, and evolutionary investigations* (pp. 199-226).

Chawla, L., & Hart, R. A. (1995). The Roots of Environmental Concern. *NAMTA Journal, 20*(1), 148-157.

Clark, A., McQuail, S., & Moss, P. (2003). *Exploring the field of listening to and consulting with young children* (Vol. 445): DfES Publications London.

Clark, A., & Moss, P. (2001). *Listening to young children: the Mosaic approach:* Ncb.

Cobb, E. (1977). The ecology of imagination in childhood: Columbia University Press (New York).

Cohen, M. J. (1983). *Prejudice against nature: a guidebook for the liberation of self and planet:* Cobblesmith.

Cornell, J. B. (1998). *Sharing nature with children:* Dawn Publications (CA).

Cosco, N. (2007). Developing Evidence-Based Design: Environmental Interventions For Healthy Development of Young Children in the Outdoors. In C. Ward-Thompson & P. Travlou (Eds.), *Open space: people space. London:* Taylor & Francis.

Devall, W. (1984). A sense of earth wisdom. *Journal of Environmental Education, 16*(2), 1-3.

DfES. (2007). *Early Years Foundation Stage.*

Dighe, J. (1993). Children and the Earth. *Young Children, 48*(3), 58-63.

Fjortoft, I. (2004). Landscape as Playscape: the effects of natural environments on children's play and motor development. Children, *Youth and Environments, 14*(2), 21-44.

Gardner, H. (1999). *Intelligence reframed: Multiple intelligences for the 21st century:* Basic Books (AZ).

Gibson, J. J. (1979). *The ecological approach to visual perception.* New Jersey: Laurence Erlbaum.

Gill, T. (2007). *No fear: Growing up in a risk averse society. London:* Caloustie Gulbenkian Foundation.

Hart, R., & Hart, R. A. (1997). Children's participation: *The theory and practice of involving young citizens in community development and environmental care:* Earthscan/James & James.

Heerwagen, J. H., & Orians, G. H. (2002). The ecological world of children. In P. Kahn & S. Kellert (Eds.), *Children and nature: Psychological, sociocultural, and evolutionary investigations* (pp. 29-64). Cambridge: MIT Press.

Hinchman, H. (1991). *A life in hand: Creating the illuminated journal:* Peregrine Smith Books.

Jersild, A. T. (2007). Children's fears. United States: Jersild Press.

Johnson, J. E., Christie, J. F., Yawkey, T. D., & Wardle, F. P. (Eds.). (1987). *Play and early childhood development.* New York: Harper Collins Publishers.

Kahn, P. H. (1999). *The human relationship with nature: Development and culture:* The MIT Press.

Kahn, P. H., & Kellert, S. R. (Eds.). (2002). *Children and nature: Psychological, sociocultural, and evolutionary investigations.* Cambridge: The MIT Press.

Kals, E., Schumacher, D., & Montada, L. (1999). Emotional affinity toward nature as a motivational basis to protect nature. *Environment and Behavior, 31*(2), 178-202.

Kaplan, R., & Kaplan, S. (1989). *The experience of nature: A psychological perspective:* Cambridge Univ Pr.

Keeler, R. (2008). *Natural playscapes: Creating outdoor play environments for the soul:* Exchange Press.

Kellert, S. R. (2002). Experiencing nature: Affective, cognitive, and evaluative development in children. In P. H. Kahn & S. R. Kellert (Eds.), *Children and nature: Psychological, sociocultural, and evolutionary investigations* (pp. 117-151): MIT Press.

Kirkby, M. (1989). Nature as refuge in children's environments. *Children's Environments Quarterly, 6*(1), 7-12.

Kytta, M. (2002). Affordances of children's environments in the context of cities, small towns, suburbs and rural villages in Finland and Belarus. *Journal of environmental psychology, 22*(1-2), 109-123.

Kytta, M. (2004). The extent of children's independent mobility and the number of actualized affordances as criteria for child-friendly environments. *Journal of environmental psychology, 24*(2), 179-198.

Kytta, M. (2006). Environmental child-friendliness in the light of the Bullerby Model. *Children and their environments: Learning, using and designing spaces,* 141-160.

Lester, S., & Maudsley, M. (2007). *Play, naturally: A review of children's natural play:* Ncb.

Lester, S., Russell, W., England, P., & Bureau, N. C. s. (2008). *Play for a change: play, policy, and practice: a review of contemporary perspectives:* Play England London.

Louv, R. (2005). *Last child in the woods: saving our children from nature-deficit disorder:* Algonquin Books.

Macfarlane, R. (2007). *The wild places:* Penguin Group USA.

Millward, A., & Wheway, R. (1998). Facilitating play on housing estates. York: Joseph Rowntree Foundation.

Moore, R. C. (1986). *Childhood's domain: Play and place in child development:* Croom Helm London.

Moore, R. C., & Cosco, N. (2000). *Developing an Earth-bound culture through design of childhood habitats.*

Moore, R. C., & Wong, H. H. (1997). *Natural learning: the life history of an environmental schoolyard: creating environments for rediscovering nature's way of teaching:* MIG communications.

Mortlock, C. (2000). *The adventure alternative.* Cumbria: Cicerone Press Limited.

Nabhan, G. (1994). A child's sense of wildness. In G. Nabhan & S. Trimble (Eds.), *The geography of childhood: Why children need wild places* (pp. 3-14). Boston: Beacon Press.

Nabhan, G. P., & Trimble, S. (Eds.). (1994). *The Geography of Childhood: Why Children Need Wild Places.* Boston: Beacon Press.

Nichols, G. (2000). Risk and adventure education. *Journal of Risk Research, 3*(2), 121-134.

Nicholson, S. (1972). *How not to cheat children: the Theory of Loose Parts:* Landscape Architecture.

Nutbrown, C. (2006). *Threads of thinking: Young children learning and the role of early education* (3rd ed.): Sage Publications Ltd.

O'Brien, L., & Murray, R. (2006). *A marvellous opportunity for children to learn: a participatory evaluation of Forest School in England and Wales* Farnham: The Forestry Commission and New Economics Foundation. .

Ollin, R. (2008). Silent pedagogy and rethinking classroom practice: structuring teaching through silence rather than talk. *Cambridge Journal of Education, 38*(2), 265-280.

Orr, D. W. (1992). *Ecological literacy: Education and the transition to a postmodern world:* State Univ of New York Pr.

Orr, D. W. (2004). *Earth in mind: On education, environment, and the human prospect:* Island Pr.

Pere, R. (1991). *Te wheke. A celebration of infinite wisdom.* Gisborne: Ao Ako Global Publishing.

Peterson, N. J. (1982). *Developmental variables affecting environmental sensitivity in professional environmental educators.* Southern Illinois University at Carbondale.

Pierce, J. (1977). Magical child: Rediscovering nature's plan for our children. *New York: DP Dutton.*

Pyle, R. M. (1993). *Thunder Tree: Lessons from an Urban Wildland.*

Pyle, R. M. (2002). Eden in a vacant lot: special places, species, and kids in the neighborhood of life. In P. H. Kahn & S. R. Kellert (Eds.), *Children and nature: Psychological, sociocultural, and evolutionary investigations* (pp. 307-327): MIT Press.

Raglon, R. (1993). Viewpoint: Reading the World: Overt and Covert Learning in Environmental Writing for Children. *The Journal of Environmental Education, 24*(4), 4-7.

Robinson, K. (2011). *Out of our minds: Learning to be creative:* Capstone.

Sandseter, E. B. H. (2009). Affordances for risky play in preschool: The importance of features in the play environment. *Early Childhood Education Journal, 36*(5), 439-446.

Sebba, R. (1991). The landscapes of childhood. *Environment and Behavior, 23*(4), 395-422.

Shaw-Jones, M. A. (1992). *Ecological worldviews: An exploratory study of the narratives of environmental studies students, or, Hearts and minds: Knowing our place in the world.* (PhD Unpublished), Antioch University.

Slade, A. (1991). *A developmental sequence for the ecological self.* (Unpublished Masters Thesis), University of Montana.

Sobel, D. (1993). *Children's special places: exploring the role of forts, dens, and bush houses in middle childhood:* Zephyr Pr Learning Materials.

Spencer, C., & Blades, M. (2006). *Children and their environments: learning, using and designing spaces:* Cambridge Univ Pr.

Tanner, T. (1980). Significant life experiences: A new research area in environmental education. *The Journal of Environmental Education, 11*(4), 20-24.

Taylor, A. F., Kuo, F. E., & Sullivan, W. C. (2001). Coping with ADD: The Surprising Connection to Green Play Settings. *Environment and Behavior, 33*(1), 54-77.

Trimble, S., & Nabhan, G. (1994). The geography of childhood: Boston, MA: Beacon Press.

Ward, C. (1988). *The child in the country:* Hale.

Warden, C. (2005). *The Potential of a Puddle:* Mindstretchers Ltd.

Warden, C. (2006). *Talking and Thinking Floorbooks: Using Big Book Planners to Consult Children*: Mindstretchers Ltd.

Warden, C. (2011). *Fascinations:* Earth. Mindstretchers Ltd.

Warden, C., & Buchan, N. (2007). *Nurture Through Nature* Mindstretchers Ltd.

Warden, C., & Spurway, K. (2002). The Right to be *"Me"*: Mindstretchers Ltd.

Williams, J. (2004). Papa-tua-nuku. Attitudes to land. In T. Ka'ai (Ed.), *Ki te whaiao: An introduction to Māori culture and society.* Auckland: Pearson Education.

Wilson, E. O. (1984). *Biophilia*: Harvard University Press.

Wilson, E. O. (1992). *The diversity of life.* New York: Springer.

Wilson, R. A. (2008). *Nature and young children: encouraging creative play and learning in natural environments:* Psychology Press.

"Tell me... What is it you plan to do
with your one wild and precious life?"

Mary Oliver